MAP
MYSTERIES

GRADES 4–6

Written by Mark Falstein • Illustrated by Kelly Kennedy

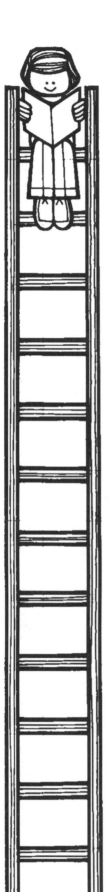

The Learning Works

LW 367

ISBN: 0-88160-297-3

Contents

Contents
(continued)

To the Teacher

Map Mysteries is designed to acquaint students in grades 4 through 6 with United States geography in an engaging and entertaining manner. Each of these two- or three-page activities contains geographical clues to 10 locations, which students must find with the help of a map or atlas. The locations may be large cities or small towns, states, or geographical features. All 50 states are represented. Where a location appears in more than one activity in the book, different geographical clues are used to guide the students to it in each instance.

In the easiest activities, clues are independent of one another, and each one points to a specific location. Other activities contain progressive clues: the student must correctly identify one place name in order to use the next clue. Several of the activities feature the additional motivation of "mystery locations," which students may be able to identify before they reach the final clue through progressive hints given in earlier clues.

Map skills, particularly the skills of interpreting directions, decoding symbols, and using a scale, are the chief objectives of *Map Mysteries*. But since the puzzlers often require students to resolve ambiguities, apply deduction, and synthesize information, the activities will stimulate their higher-level thinking skills as well.

The primary clues for an easily found map location are typically given in terms of direction and distance from the place students identified in the previous clue (e.g., "About 75 miles southeast of here . . ."; "About 60 miles south and a little west . . ."; "About 200 miles due south"). Most clues are deliberately unspecific in this manner, as precise distances are all but impossible to determine with a standard map scale, and precise directions can be conveyed only by the use of degree headings. Accordingly, secondary clues are given: locations relative to bodies of water, state borders, and other nearby map features. In some cases, where students are asked to locate a small town or city among many place names within a relatively small area, a tertiary clue is given (e.g., "The name of the town has seven letters, beginning with 'A'"). Most clues contain an interesting or unusual fact about the location, as well. Place and feature names used in *Map Mysteries* can be found in most standard atlases, and all can be found in the maps included in articles on the respective states in *World Book Encyclopedia*.

On the last page of each mystery, lines are provided for students to write in the answer to each clue. An answer key is provided on pages 91-96.

To the Teacher
(continued)

Contents

The book is divided into five sections, though the activities need not be presented in any particular order.

Regional Mysteries: Each of these five activities focuses on a specific geographical region of the United States: the Northeast, Southeast, Midwest, Near West, and Far West.

Cross-Curriculum Mysteries: These nine activities call on students to identify geographical locations associated with historical events, works of literature, scientific achievements, and items of note in other curriculum areas. In one mathematics-based activity, the clues are given as latitude and longitude coordinates.

Geographical Features: In these four activities, the clues point to state capitals as well as land features such as mountains, prairies, islands, and bodies of water.

General Mysteries: These four activities have no specific theme, and all are framed by a lightly treated "mystery" storyline, such as a hunt for hidden gold or the pursuit of a thief.

Just For Fun: These last five activities call on students to identify geographic locations associated with inventions, national parks, monuments and memorials, the world of sports, and local festivals.

As a whole-class activity: Students can solve a Map Mystery as a group, with individuals being called upon to solve the clues using a wall map or pull-down map of the United States.

If detailed maps of the states and the United States are available in student geography texts or atlases, students may be assigned an activity as desk work. Completed activity sheets may be placed in students' file folders or portfolios.

As a learning-center activity: Small groups of students may be given an activity to complete cooperatively at a learning center, using an atlas or other appropriate reference. To provide additional motivation, hold time trials of various groups on successful completion of an activity, and devise a point system for order of finish for a class competition.

As an extra-credit or homework activity: Students can be assigned activities to complete using available references at home or in the school or public library. Completed activity sheets may be placed in students' file folders or portfolios.

Regional Mysteries

Exploring the Northeastern States

"Okay, Mom, what about this 'sweet treat' you promised us?" Laurel Tandy asked from the back seat.

"Yeah, Mom," her brother Anthony said. "Are we going to be there in time for lunch?"

"You'll have to wait a little longer than that," their mother said. "We're going to Aunt Esther and Uncle Paul's, and you know that's a long trip. Meanwhile, let's make a game of it. See if you can guess where and what that treat will be."

1. The Tandys had left Washington, D.C., that morning. They drove through Annapolis, Maryland, crossed a bridge over Chesapeake Bay, and headed northeast into Delaware. "Just ahead is this state's biggest city," Mrs. Tandy said. "It's on the Delaware River, just northeast of New Castle. Can you find its name on a map? It begins with a 'W.'"

2. The Tandys crossed another bridge, going east. Now they were in New Jersey. "About 75 miles southeast of here is a famous beach resort named for the ocean it faces," Mrs. Tandy said. "A man named Charles Darrow once lived there. He invented the game 'Monopoly.' The names of the streets in the game are taken from that city."

   "I know what city you mean," Laura said. "Are we going to have salt-water taffy? Is that the treat you mean?"

   "No, there won't be any salt water in the treat," her mother said.

3. The Tandys crossed the Hudson River a little north of New York City. That evening, they stopped in Connecticut for the night. "Why is this town named for a city in England?" Anthony asked.

   "Because that's where the first European settlers came from," his mother said. "That river, the Thames, is also named for a river in England. Right across the river is Groton, where submarines are made for the United States Navy."

4. The next day the Tandys drove northeast through Massachusetts. They had dinner about 35 miles northeast of Boston. It was in a city at the north end of Massachusetts Bay. The name of the city has 10 letters, beginning with the letter "G." "This is a great fish dinner," Laura said, "But it can't be the treat you promised us."

   "No, for that you'll have to wait until we drive back through Pennsylvania," her mother said.

5. Mrs. Tandy's sister Esther and her family owned a boat store. It was in Maine's largest city, on Casco Bay, about 50 miles southwest of the state capital. "Aunt Esther, you make a great peach pie," said Anthony, with his mouth full. "Mom, is that treat going to be better than this?"

   "Not better," said Mrs. Tandy, "but darker."

6. After their visit, the Tandys took the long way home. They crossed New Hampshire going northwest. They stopped at Franconia Notch to see "The Old Man of the Mountains." (This is a rock formation that looks like a man's face.) They stayed that night in a town 15 miles northwest of there, on the Connecticut River. "This sure is a 'little town,'" Laura joked.

7. The next morning, the Tandys crossed the Connecticut River and headed west. They drove through the nation's smallest state capital. About 40 miles northwest of there, they stopped at a city on Lake Champlain. Its name starts with the letter "B" and has 10 letters. "Ethan Allan, the Revolutionary War hero, is buried here," Mrs. Tandy said, "but other heroes lived here too. The city was a stop on the Underground Railroad."

8. The Tandys took a ferry across Lake Champlain. Then they followed the Hudson River south until they came to a city a little beyond the place where the Hudson was joined by the Mohawk River. "This is an interesting city," Ms. Tandy said. "It dates back to 1624, and was a trading place for Native Americans long before that. Now it's a state capital. But we turn west here."

9. In Pennsylvania, the Tandys found themselves driving behind a family in a horse-drawn wagon. "What a neat way to get around!" Anthony exclaimed.

"And it's good for the environment," Laura added.

"Those people are Old-Order Amish," their mother said. "They're a religious group that came here long ago from Germany. They've kept many of their old ways. Many of them live near a city that's about 65 miles west of Philadelphia and 40 miles southeast of Harrisburg. Maybe you can find it on the map. It has the same name as the county it's in."

10. "Speaking of the map," Laura said, "I think I've figured out what the treat is. Does it have to do with kisses and chocolate bars and a town that's about 15 miles east of Harrisburg?"

"Yes, it does," her mother said with a smile.

"We're going to tour the world's biggest chocolate factory!" Laura told her brother.

Can you name the places the Tandys visited or talked about? Write the city and state names below.

1. _____   6. _____

2. _____   7. _____

3. _____   8. _____

4. _____   9. _____

5. _____   10. _____

A Southeastern Treasure Hunt

"Follow these directions," the old map read, "and you will find gold." At least it *looked* like an old map. I had found it hidden in a book. I had a sneaking suspicion that the whole thing was a practical joke. But since I'm a travel writer for magazines, I thought there might be a story in it.

1. I'd found the book at a public library in my hometown. I live in the state that is sometimes called the "mother of presidents" because four of the first five were born here. My town is 20 miles south of Richmond, the state capital. Its name begins with the letter "P." It's famous for having been besieged by the Union Army during the Civil War, and it's the home of a national battlefield.

2. The first instructions were to go south and west to a city in North Carolina. With Raleigh, 25 miles southeast of there, and Chapel Hill, about 12 miles southwest, it forms the state's famed "research triangle." Duke University is there, and so is a famous minor-league baseball team. The city's name is the same as its county.

3. "Head southeast to a city by the sea," the map said. "Then go about 150 miles southwest to an old city on a big harbor." The 'city by the sea' was Wilmington. The 'old city by a big harbor' could only mean one place. It was across another state line, on a peninsula where three rivers empty into the Atlantic. In its harbor is Fort Sumter, where the Civil War began.

4. I went west across the Savannah River and into another state. The directions said to cross that state westward to a city named for a famous explorer. It was easy to find. It's right across the Chattahoochee River from Phenix City, Alabama.

5. From there it was only a little more than 40 miles west to the next place the directions told me to go. Its name has eight letters starting with "T." It's the home of a famous African-American university, founded by Booker T. Washington. The great scientist George Washington Carver did his experiments there.

6. Next I traveled southwest to the oldest city in Alabama. It's the hometown of baseball great Henry Aaron. It's a seaport, located on a bay and a river with the same name as the city.

7. I drove west, out of Alabama and across the southern end of another state. Then I found myself in the only state in the Union named after a king of France. I spent the night in its capital, whose name is French for "red stick." It's on the Mississippi River, about 75 miles northwest of New Orleans. "Hmm," I thought, "there's a lot of oil in this state. Oil is so valuable, it's sometimes called 'black gold.' Could that mean something?"

8. But, no. My instructions were to head north, into the home state of our 37th president, Bill Clinton. I spent the night in the strangest national park I've ever heard of. It's about 55 miles southwest of the state capital, and it's entirely surrounded by a city. Both the park and city are named for the water that gushes out of the ground here.

9. The next day I was heading east again. I crossed the Mississippi at Memphis and continued on northeast another 200 miles. Here was a city I'd been wanting to visit for a long time. It's a state capital—but it's also the country music capital of the world. I toured the Grand Ole Opry that afternoon and took in a Garth Brooks concert that night.

10. One more leg to my journey. I drove north and crossed into another state. The directions said to go north to Elizabethtown, take the left-hand fork in the road, and go another 17 miles.

   I found the gold, all right. A lot of good it did me. The directions led me to—Fort Knox! That's where the U.S. government keeps its gold. It may be the world's best-protected vault. Feeling like a fool, I ended my trip in the state's largest city, 25 miles northeast of there. "Oh well," I thought, "it was a nice trip. And maybe I *would* get a story out of it."

Can you name all the places the writer visited? Write the city and state names below.

1. _____   6. _____

2. _____   7. _____

3. _____   8. _____

4. _____   9. _____

5. _____   10. _____

In the Heart of the Country

Good evening and welcome to everybody's *favorite* game show, "Mystery Town." Tonight we feature 10 individuals from the middle of the country. Name the cities and states where these people hail from, and *you* may be eligible for our next super-gigantic "Mystery Town" jackpot! Are your pencils and paper ready? Now, pay attention as our 10 guests give you clues about their hometowns.

Guest 1: The name of my hometown sounds like it involves driving. It's an industrial city on the Ohio River, in the heart of coal-mining country. It's about 20 miles south of Steubenville, Ohio, and less than 15 miles from Pennsylvania, but it's neither in Ohio nor Pennsylvania.

Guest 2: I live in a city on Lake Michigan. It's about 90 miles north of Chicago and about 75 miles east of our state's capital. It became home to the country's first kindergarten in 1856, and has one of the finest natural history museums in the United States. A lot of German people settled here in the 1800s, and it's a center for German-American culture.

Guest 3: I come from a state known for its farms. The Mississippi River borders the state on the east, but my city is at the western edge of the state. It's at the borders of two other states, but you have to cross rivers to get to them. My town was named after a Native American people. It's about 235 miles west of Waterloo. The biggest popcorn-processing plant in the United States is located there, so it's a snack-lover's dream.

Guest 4: Do you like cereal for breakfast? Then you should come to my hometown. Cereal processing is the town's biggest industry, and you can tour the factories and take home samples. The town is about midway between Marshall and Kalamazoo, and about 70 miles northeast of South Bend, Indiana.

Guest 5: I guess there's a theme here. My city processes farm produce, too. It also has a lot of manufacturing. Those automatic bank-teller machines are just one of the products that are made here. But the city is best known as the home of the Pro Football Hall of Fame. The National Football League was organized here in 1920, in a car dealership. My hometown is located in the state between Indiana and Pennsylvania. It's about 20 miles southeast of Akron and less than 10 miles east of Massillon.

Guest 6: You've got football—we've got basketball! A lot of great basketball players have come from my state. In fact, the great Boston Celtics' star Larry Bird played college basketball in my hometown! The name of the town is French for "high ground." It's built on bluffs over the Wabash River. It's located about 150 miles south of Gary, which is at the southern end of Lake Michigan, and only a few miles from the Illinois line.

Guest 7: Funny you should mention basketball; my city was the original home of the Los Angeles Lakers. Have you ever wondered how they got the name "Lakers"? Well, the name made sense when they played for my city because 22 lakes lie within the city limits. We're across the Mississippi River from St. Paul, and the two places are known as "the twin cities." Go east about 25 miles, and you're in Wisconsin.

Guest 8: I live in the same state as guest number five, about 60 miles northwest. It's the biggest city in the state, an old manufacturing center on Lake Erie. The Cuyahoga River runs through the center of town. The river used to be so polluted with chemicals that it once actually caught fire! Just 30 miles west along the lakefront is Lorain, hometown of the Nobel prize-winning writer Toni Morrison.

Guest 9: My city is a state capital, and it's named for a president of the United States. It's about halfway between the state's two biggest cities, and it lies on a river with the same name as the state. I'll give you another hint. You can drive through my state to get to Oklahoma, Nebraska, or Tennessee.

Guest 10: Saved the best for last, did you? My city's in the northeast corner of my state. It's not the state capital. It's more like the capital of the whole Midwest! Just look at a map and you'll see where all the highways and railroads go. And we've got the world's busiest airport, too. We're—let's see—300 miles northeast of St. Louis, 300 miles west of Detroit, and 400 miles southeast of Minneapolis. And I've got just two words to say to all of you sports fans: Michael Jordan!

How did you do in the "Mystery Town" game? Write the names of the cities and states below.

1. _____
2. _____
3. _____
4. _____
5. _____

6. _____
7. _____
8. _____
9. _____
10. _____

Where the West Begins

Look at a map of the United States. Imagine a line running south from Canada, passing along the western borders of Minnesota, Iowa, Missouri, Arkansas, and Louisiana. Here is where the West begins. Hi. I'm Cowgirl Cagill. Let's take a tour of my part of the country—the Great Plains. Imagine that you're riding beside me on a horse. I hope your canteen is full, because it's going to be a long and dusty ride!

1. We start at the Mexican border. That's only right, since so much of the history and culture of the West is tied to Mexico. We're in a town on the Rio Grande, near where it enters the sea. Matamoros, Mexico is on the opposite bank.

2. We ride 260 miles north and a little west. We come to a city with a Spanish name. It's about 80 miles southwest of Austin, the state capital. In this city there is an old mission and a fort called the Alamo. A famous battle was fought here in 1836. (People around these parts are always telling you to remember it.)

3. Keep riding north, partner—a long way north, into the next state and through that state's capital. Now we turn northeast and go through the city of Tulsa. Another 20 miles, and we come to a small town whose name begins with the letter "C." It was the home of Will Rogers, the cowboy who became an entertainment star. He was famous for his "prairie wisdom," and for saying, "I never met a man I didn't like."

4. Keep riding north, until we cross into another state. Let's rest our horses at a farm community right near the middle of the state. It's the seat of Barton County, and it's named for a bend in the Arkansas River just south of the town.

5. We continue our long trail northward until we arrive in yet another state. Heading northwest, we come to the forks of the Platte River. There's a city right in the "Y" between them. It's a big railroad center. You can't miss it as it's the only place of any size for miles around.

6. Notice how the country is more sparsely populated as we ride north. There's mostly big farms and ranches around here, and not many towns. We ride past the town of Valentine and into another state. We're in Sioux country now. This is part of their reservation. From here it's 160 miles northwest to the only large city in these parts. It's the "gateway to the Black Hills" and is named for the creek that runs through it.

7. We ride north again—hope you're not getting tired! We cross into yet another state. All that's north of here is Canada—and west is the Badlands. We stop in a town that's 100 miles west of Bismarck, the state capital, and about 60 miles east of the Montana line. Its name has nine letters, beginning with "D." There's a state university here, but what you mostly see are amber waves of grain.

8. Let's ride west now, into Montana. When we reach Glendive, we follow the Yellowstone River southwest. This is a *big* state. We ride 220 miles and come to its largest city. Here you'll find the state's tallest building—18 stories high. The Crow Indian Reservation is just southeast of here.

9. Now we turn south, into still another state. We follow the trail south to Riverton. Then we turn northwest and cross the Rocky Mountains. We rest for a spell at a resort town with the same name as a president. It's just east of the Snake River and just south of Grand Teton National Park.

10. Let's follow the Snake River westward. Soon we're in Idaho. This is rough country. South of Blackfoot and old Fort Hall we come to a city of some size on the Portneuf River. It's a market and shipping point for the farm products of this region.

    Thanks for joining me, partner. I figure we've been in the saddle more than 3,000 miles. You'd better think twice before going on north, into Salmon River country. They don't call it "the river of no return" for nothing!

Can you name the places where you stopped? Write the city and state names below.

1. _____   6. _____

2. _____   7. _____

3. _____   8. _____

4. _____   9. _____

5. _____   10. _____

Ocean, Mountain, Desert: The Far West

Hey, there. I'm Sourdough Joe. I'll be your guide through the states of the far west. We'll go by airplane. Where I come from, small planes like the one I fly are sometimes the only way in and out of places.

1. We'll start in my hometown. It's on the northwest coast of Norton Sound, near the western edge of my state. In fact, it's about as far west as you can go and still be in the United States. Russia is located to the west just across the Bering Sea. A famous race is held each year, called the Iditarod, that starts in Anchorage, southeast of here, and ends up in my town. That's about 570 miles by plane, but the Iditarod racers go by dogsled!

2. We fly south from my home—more than 3,000 miles over the sea. We come to a chain of islands. They're not part of continental America, but they are part of the United States. We land in the harbor of the state's largest city. It's on the south shore of Oahu Island.

3. We fly northeast, back toward the mainland. I've had enough water for now! After we refuel, we head for the desert.

   We pass over a spot where the corners of four states meet—Arizona, New Mexico, Utah, and Colorado. From there we fly about 35 miles northeast and land near a town named for the Spanish soldier who conquered Mexico. There are some fascinating Native American ruins at Mesa Verde National Park, about 10 miles southeast of here.

4. Next we head south, about 165 miles, into another state. When we see the Zuñi Pueblo below us, we turn east and fly another 120 miles to this state's largest city, named for a Spanish duke who ruled this area in the 1700s. It's about 50 miles southwest of Santa Fe, the state capital.

5. We go west now and fly over the next state we come to. We fly over the Petrified Forest, the Hopi Reservation, and the Grand Canyon. We stop for gas at a city near the western border of the state. It's about 150 miles west of Flagstaff and less than 30 miles east of Bullhead City.

6. From there we fly about 90 miles northwest, over Hoover Dam and Lake Mead and into another state. Wow—look at all the bright lights down there! That could only be one city. It's one of the fastest-growing cities in the United States. Do you know about the hotel there that looks like an Egyptian pyramid?

7. Let's find a quieter place to refuel. We fly northeast, over a corner of Arizona, and into another state. The town I have in mind is named for a tree. It's about 30 miles north of Zion National Park and about 50 miles northeast of St. George.

8. Now we head west, across the state of Nevada. We cross into California and fly over Yosemite National Park. Then we continue due west, about 170 miles, to a city that's at the end of a peninsula. To the west is the Pacific Ocean. To the north and east is a bay with the same name as the city. Be careful if you land here—it's earthquake country! (Of course, the same can be said for most of the Pacific coast.)

9. It's time to head for home. We fly due north, until we just cross into another state. See that pretty little town down there? A theater festival is held there every summer. People come from all over the country to see actors perform plays. It's about 10 miles southeast of Medford and about 45 miles west of Klamath Falls. It's name begins with an "A."

10. We continue north into Washington. Our next stop will be a city on Puget Sound. It's about 25 miles northeast of the state capital and about 35 miles south of the state's largest city.

    And that's about as far as we go. I've got to head on back to Alaska, but you can stay here in the "lower 48" and keep warm. I hope you've enjoyed exploring the far-western states.

Can you name all the places where you stopped? Write the city and state names below.

1. _____   6. _____

2. _____   7. _____

3. _____   8. _____

4. _____   9. _____

5. _____   10. _____

Cross-Curriculum Mysteries

Find the Monument

A cross marks the spot where Jacques Marquette, the French priest and explorer of North America, spent the winter before he died in 1675. Can you name the place where this monument can be found? Of course you can—but first, you must find your way to some other sites that figured in America's early history.

1. Marquette certainly passed this way. You're near a town in Illinois, across the Mississippi River from St. Louis, Missouri. Its name has seven letters, beginning with "C." You're in a state park with the same name as the town. In the 1100s about 30,000 people lived here, but this Native American trading center was long gone by the time Marquette passed this way.

2. Now travel southeast, to the state of Florida. About 35 miles southeast of Jacksonville is the oldest European-founded city in the United States. This city, founded in 1565 by the Spanish, is named for a saint.

3. Follow the Atlantic coast northward. Cross one state border, then another. Now turn northwest. Follow the Savannah River about 180 miles. Go east through the towns of Abbeville and Greenwood. You'll find a town with a name that is a two-digit number. A Revolutionary War battle was fought here in 1780. But this state was an English colony; the French were never here.

4. Continue east, back to the Atlantic coast. You'll cross one state border on the way; now turn north along the coast and cross another. Between the James River and the York River, about 35 miles northwest of Norfolk, is a restored colonial village. It looks like it could have been here in 1675, but it is far to the east and south of Marquette's explorations. Besides, you're looking for a much larger city.

5. Let's try a different part of the country. Go west to Texas. Then continue west into the next state. Here you'll find the oldest state capital in the United States. It was founded in 1610. But the name of the river west of here—the Rio Grande—tells you that this area was settled by the Spanish, not the French. There's a river at our final destination, but it isn't *grande*—and it flows uphill!

6. Let's go back east, to New Jersey. About 25 miles east and a little north of the state capital is a monument to Molly Pitcher. She was a heroine of a Revolutionary War battle fought here in 1778. Although the town is now named Freehold, it used to have the same name as the county and the battlefield. It begins with the letter "M." But we're nowhere near the territory explored by Marquette.

7. Now go west. Cross the Delaware River, not far from where George Washington's army crossed it in 1776. Follow the river southwest about 35 miles to a large city. Ben Franklin lived here and so did Dolley Madison—but not Father Marquette.

8. Stay in the same state. Go to its western part, where the Allegheny and Monongahela rivers meet to form the Ohio River. You're getting warmer! The French were the first Europeans to explore this part of the country. The first European settlement on this spot was a French fort—Fort Duquesne (du-KANE). But it was not built until 1754.

9. Now go north. You'll come to one of the Great Lakes. You'll need a boat now. Follow the waterways west and north into another Great Lake. Continue traveling in a northwesterly direction until you pass between Bois Blanc and Mackinac islands. Here, on the other side of a bridge from Mackinaw City, Michigan, was a trading post where the French bought furs from Native Americans. In fact, it was the place Marquette was trying to reach when he died.

10. Now you know you're getting close. Go southwest into yet another Great Lake. In its far southwest corner, you'll find a large city. (It's in the same state where we started.) In this city, on a river with the same name as the city, is the spot where Jean Baptiste Pointe du Sable built his trading post in the 1770s. Not far away is the Marquette Cross. It marks the site of the cabin where he spent his last winter.

Can you name all the places you visited? Write the names of the cities and states on the lines below.

1. _____   6. _____

2. _____   7. _____

3. _____   8. _____

4. _____   9. _____

5. _____   10. _____

On the Trail of the Great and the Near-Great

"Mother, I've decided how I'm going to spend my summer vacation," Arnelle Wilson announced.

"And how is that?" her mother asked.

"I'm going to research the life of a great American for my senior-class history report. There are a lot of people I'm interested in."

"Why, that's wonderful," said Sally's mother. "I suppose you'll be spending a lot of time in the library."

"Oh, no, mother," Sally said. "I want to personally visit the places these people lived and worked. That's the only way to do research. May I borrow the car for the summer?"

1. "First, I'll visit the home of Dr. Martin Luther King, Jr. There's an information center there where I can learn more about how he led the fight for African-American civil rights in the 1950s and 1960s. It's in a big city in Fulton County, Georgia, on the Chattahoochee River. Some people call it 'the Capital of the South.'"

2. "Then I'll go northwest, to Chattanooga, and then due west to a city on the Mississippi River. That's where Graceland is—Elvis Presley's home. Of course, he was one of the greatest singers in the history of rock and roll music! W. C. Handy, another great musician who was known as 'the Father of the Blues,' lived and worked here, too."

3. "Of course, I might choose to write about Susan B. Anthony. She was a leader of the movement for equal rights for women in the 1800s. I'll go to the city in New York where she was arrested for voting in 1872. It's on Lake Ontario, about 100 miles northwest of Syracuse."

4. "While I'm in New York, I'll visit the home of Harriet Tubman. She escaped from slavery in 1849 and later helped about 300 other slaves to escape. She spent her later years in this New York town. It's at the northern end of Owasco Lake, about 25 miles southwest of Syracuse. The name of the town begins with an 'A,' and is a word used to describe a certain hair color."

5. "I've always wanted to see New Mexico because I'm interested in the famous American artist Georgia O'Keeffe. She settled in a town near this cool Native American pueblo. The name of this place slips my mind, but it's very short and begins with the letter 'T.' It's more than 1,000 years old! It's in the Sangre de Cristo mountains, about 55 miles northeast of Santa Fe."

6. "While I'm in the West, I'll go to the state that's north of Nevada and west of Idaho. Near the northeastern corner of the state is a town called Enterprise. Just southeast of there, on Lake Wallowa, is a town named for a Native American leader. He was a Nez Percé chief who led his people on a famous retreat in 1877. When he finally gave himself up to the United States Army, he said, 'I will fight no more forever.' Maybe I'll do my report on him."

7. "On the other hand, maybe I'll do it on General Ulysses S. Grant. When we studied the Civil War last year, we learned about one of the battles that he won. It took place in a southern state, just east of Louisiana. He captured a city about 40 miles west of Jackson, the state capital. The city is on a river with the same name as the state."

8. "Speaking of the Civil War, maybe I'll choose Harriet Beecher Stowe. After all, her book, *Uncle Tom's Cabin*, helped turn the North against Southern slavery. She wrote it in a town in Maine. The town has nine letters in its name. It's about seven miles west of the town of Bath, and about 25 miles northeast of Portland."

9. "Or maybe I'll write about Babe Ruth, the famous baseball player. He played major-league ball in New York and Boston, but he was born in a city on the Chesapeake Bay. It's about 40 miles northeast of Washington, D.C., and about 25 miles north of Annapolis, Maryland."

10. "I have an idea," Arnelle's mother said. "You could write about Sarah Goddard. She was the one of first women to publish a newspaper in America, in 1765."

    "That sounds interesting," said Arnelle. "Where did she live?"

    "In a city in New England. It's a state capital, about 50 miles southwest of Boston, Massachusetts."

    "But that sounds like our city," Arnelle replied.

    "It is," said her mother with a smile. "So you won't need the car after all!"

Can you name the cities and states Arnelle planned to visit? Write their names on the lines below. Be sure to write the name of her city as number 10.

1. _____   6. _____

2. _____   7. _____

3. _____   8. _____

4. _____   9. _____

5. _____   10. _____

Finding Lily Lightfoot

Professor Lily Lightfoot was difficult to locate—and it was my job to find her. My name is Paul Grant and I work for the Spendwell Foundation. The foundation wanted to award Lily $100,000 for her research on Native American cultures. The trouble was, we couldn't find her. My only clue was a photograph she had sent me a while back. In the photo, she was standing in front of a huge totem pole. Freshly caught salmon were hanging nearby. Clearly, she was in some Native American village. But where?

1. I showed the picture to some residents of a town northeast of the Seminole Reservation. The town is located on (and shares the name of) a large lake southwest of Fort Pierce, Florida, where the Seminole hunted and fished. Some women in colorful tribal costumes grinned and nudged each other. "You'd better go north, stranger," one of them said. "*Way* north," said another.

2. So I did. I went to a large city at the mouth of the Hudson River. I could see Jersey City, New Jersey, on the opposite bank. I had a good view of it because I was on the 50th floor of a skyscraper! I was with some workers of the Mohawk nation. Most of the Mohawk today live in Canada, but their people have long been involved in high-rise construction in this city. It's about 160 miles south of their ancestors' lands. They also laughed when I showed them the picture. "You'd better go west," one said. "*Way* west."

3. On a hunch, I went to a town in Highland County, Ohio. Near this town, about halfway between Cincinnati and Chillicothe, is a place called Great Serpent Mound. It's a big, curving snake made of earth, about four feet high and a quarter-mile long. Native Americans built it hundreds of years ago. But I didn't see any totem poles nearby. The name of the town has nine letters, beginning with "H."

4. I headed northwest, to Chippewa country. The Chippewa belong to one of the largest native tribes in North America. "You'd better keep traveling," said a man in a cafe. We were in a city just across the Red River from Fargo, North Dakota. "We're a woodland people. There are neither totem poles nor salmon around here."

5. I was getting nowhere fast. The Navajo is *the* largest tribe in the United States, so I headed for Navajo country. Many Navajo still tend sheep in the high desert like their ancestors did. But their capital is a modern town. It's in Arizona, on its eastern border, just south of Fort Defiance. It's named for a large rock that has a hole through it. I saw beautiful woolen rugs and turquoise jewelry, but no totem poles. "You're looking for a place a lot cooler and wetter than this desert," a Navajo told me.

6. I was getting desperate. I went to the state north of Texas, to the capital of the Cherokee nation. The city I visited is the county seat of Cherokee County, in the eastern part of the state. "You're lost, stranger," a farmer told me. "I don't think you'll find your friend here."

7. I headed northwest about 55 miles to the state's second-largest city. Native Americans of many tribes work in the oil fields here. I was near the birthplace of Maria Tallchief, the famous Osage ballet dancer. Jim Thorpe, the great athlete of the Sac-and-Fox tribe, was also born near here. But there was still no sign of Lily.

8. I traveled to a city in Montana, about 100 miles northwest of the state capital and about 50 miles east of the Idaho line. I decided to do some research on salmon at the library of the University of Montana. Not far from here, the Shoshone woman Sacajawea guided Lewis and Clark across the Rocky Mountains in 1805. I could have used a guide myself!

9. At last I was in salmon country. The Yakima people still fish the Columbia River here. We were in the only state named for a U.S. president, south of Pasco, and just a few miles west of where the Snake River joins the Columbia. The name of the town had nine letters beginning with "K." "You'd better keep going northwest," a fisherman advised me.

10. How much further northwest could I go and still be in the United States? Of course— how silly of me! I caught up with Lily in a state capital. It was just a few miles south and west of the Canadian border. "I'm living in a Tlingit village," she told me. "You should have been able to figure it out from the totem pole!"

Can you name the cities and towns where Paul looked for Lily? Write their names and the states they are located in on the lines below.

1. _____   6. _____

2. _____   7. _____

3. _____   8. _____

4. _____   9. _____

5. _____   10. _____

A Journey Through Space and Time

It is the year 2195. Megan Martinez is testing the time machine she has invented. It's a bumpy ride. Megan keeps jumping from place to place—and from time to time. "I need help," is the message she sends back to her lab by Z-wave. "My computer will tell me the date, the year, or the period of history I'm in, but not where I am. Help me out, please! I was a pretty good history student, but I was terrible in geography!"

1. "It's 1848. I'm at a big meeting for women's rights. It's in a town just east of Waterloo, New York, at the north end of Cayuga Lake. The name of the town has two words. A woman named Elizabeth Cady Stanton is addressing the crowd. I want to leave this period of history as quickly as possible. Women in this day and age aren't treated fairly at all!"

2. "Whoops! I've just been zapped clear across the country! I'm in California, during the Gold Rush. They called this place Hangtown then, but I seem to remember that it has another name now. The name of the city has 11 letters and begins with the letter 'P.' It's in the foothills of the Sierra Nevada, about 40 miles east of the state capital."

3. "Whoa! There's shooting going on here! By looking at the soldiers' uniforms, I'd say I'm in the midst of the Civil War. My control panel says 1859. That's before the war started. Wait—I have it! It's John Brown's raid! He tried to start a slave revolt by seizing an army weapons station. Let me see . . . the name of this town also has two names. It must have been a place where a boat carried passengers across the Potomac River. It's in West Virginia, right in the corner where the state joins Virginia and Maryland."

4. "More shooting! This time it's cowboys. I guess they've just driven a herd of cattle up from Texas. It's 1870. I must be in that Kansas town that was the end of the Old Chisholm Trail. It's about 25 miles east and a little north of Salina. What *is* the name of this town? Seven letters, begins with 'A'. . . ."

5. "I must be in the 20th century now. I can see Henry Ford, watching his first Model T automobile come off the assembly line. Yes, it's 1908. He set out to build a car that most Americans could afford, and that's just what he did. I'm in a suburb that joins Detroit, Michigan, on the southwest. Its name rhymes with 'gear-worn.'"

6. "Okay, here I am in Tennessee. I'm near the Tennessee River, about 35 miles northeast of Chattanooga. It's 1924. There's no shooting here, but there sure is a lot of shouting going on. Must be that famous "monkey trial" that was held after charges were brought against a teacher for giving a lecture on the Theory of Evolution. The trial caused a fuss all over the country. But what *is* the name of the town . . . ? It has the same name as a city in southwestern Ohio—six letters, beginning with 'D.'"

7. "I've landed in the middle of a war! Planes are dropping bombs on ships! My computer says it's December 7, 1941. It must be the bombing of Pearl Harbor. This event brought the United States into World War II. Pearl Harbor is in Hawaii. Honolulu's just east of there, but I'm in some little town to the northwest that begins with the letter 'W.'"

8. "What's this? The police are taking a woman off a bus. They're taking her to jail. Why, she must be Rosa Parks. It's December 1, 1955. That's the day she defied an Alabama law and refused to give up her seat on the bus for a white man. That took a lot of courage! But where are we? The city we're in is a state capital on the Alabama River, southeast of Birmingham, and west of Columbus, Georgia."

9. "Oh, no! This is terrible! It's November 22, 1963, and President John F. Kennedy has just been assassinated! I'm in Texas, in the northeastern part of the state. It's a large city 30 miles east of Fort Worth."

10. "This doesn't look good. Someone is making an angry speech. A lot of people are making angry speeches. Now they're marching, carrying signs, and chanting. My time machine computer says it's 1970. This must be a protest against the war in Vietnam. I'm in a town in California, on the east side of San Francisco Bay. I'm pretty sure the name of the town begins with the letter 'B.' I'll bet it's that university town just north of Oakland."

   "I give up. I'm bringing the time machine back home. Hey, now that I mention it—where *is* home?"

Can you identify the locations of the historical events Megan visited? Write the names of the cities and states on the lines below.

1. _____   6. _____

2. _____   7. _____

3. _____   8. _____

4. _____   9. _____

5. _____   10. _____

In the Wild

"I'm thinking of an animal," Ms. Trixter told her class. "It used to be abundant in North America, but now it's hard to find except in museums. See if you can guess the animal, and a place where you can still see it in the wild."

1. "The California condor," Juan suggested. "I saw one on a camping trip in California last summer. It was near _____ , a town named for a tree, due east of Sequoia National Park."

    "Good guess," Ms. Trixter said, "but the animal I'm thinking of comes from a place farther east and north."

2. "How about the American bison?" Lydia asked. "Hunters killed almost all of them more than 100 years ago. But I saw a herd of them once. We were staying in _____ , Colorado, where the Colorado River meets the Gunnison."

    "You're close in one sense," Ms. Trixter said. "but you're pretty far off in another sense. Hunters didn't kill off this animal."

3. "The pronghorn," Tyrone suggested. "Pronghorns are similar to antelope. Native Americans used to hunt them in the sand hills of Nebraska. I saw some at a wildlife refuge near there. We were staying in _____ . That's a town on the north bank of the North Platte River. It's just about 20 miles east of the Wyoming state line."

    "Another good guess," said Ms. Trixter. "But the animal I'm thinking of was much bigger than a pronghorn."

4. "I know! A grizzly bear!" Lynn said. "They used to be all over the country, but now they're living wild in just a few areas. I saw one when I was visiting my uncle. He lives in _____ , Wyoming. It's on the Shoshone River, about 50 miles east of the boundary of Yellowstone National Park. That bear sure was huge!"

   "Grizzlies are big," the teacher agreed, "but the species I'm thinking of was even bigger."

5. "A blue whale," Maiko offered. "Of course, you have to see them from a boat. You can join a whale-watching cruise in _____ . That's the largest city in Alaska, west of the Chugach Mountains and right at the head of Cook Inlet."

   "You're all wet," the teacher said teasingly. "I'm thinking of a land animal."

6. "You did say 'animal,' didn't you?" asked Alphonse. "If not, maybe you mean a bristlecone pine tree. They're the oldest living things on earth. You can find them in only one place, near _____ , California. That's on the Owens River, about 60 miles northwest of the place where Juan saw his condor."

   "I did say 'animal,'" Ms. Trixter said. "And it's even older than the bristlecone pine."

7. "Maybe it's an ocelot," said Sean. "There are very few of these wild cats left because they were hunted for their fur. Some of them live in the desert southeast of _____ , Arizona. That's the state's second-largest city, about 90 miles southeast of the state capital."

   "The animal I'm thinking of was a fierce predator, like the ocelot," said the teacher. "But it was never hunted for its fur."

8. "This is a wild guess," Patricia said. "But what about the whooping crane? That's a bird that was almost extinct a few years ago. There were only a few of them at the Aransas National Wildlife Refuge in Texas. That's on a bay about 50 miles northeast of _____ .

"But they've come back since then," Ms. Trixter said. "Time for another hint. The animal I'm thinking of *is* extinct."

9. "The passenger pigeon!" Darryl said. "The last one died in 1914, in a zoo in _____ , Ohio. That's a large city on the Ohio River, 20 miles east of the Indiana border."

"Good guess," said Ms. Trixter, "but it's not a bird. On the other hand, many scientists think it was a cousin of birds."

10. "Oh, you are tricky!" Dinah said. "Let me ask you this: Is the place you can see them 'in the wild' on the border between Utah and Colorado? About 75 miles west of _____ , Colorado?"

"That's right," the teacher smiled, "at Dinosaur National Monument."

"Then you must be talking about a Tyrannosaurus rex!"

"You've got it!" said Ms. Trixter.

Can you identify the cities and towns the students mentioned? Write their names on the lines below.

1. _____   6. _____

2. _____   7. _____

3. _____   8. _____

4. _____   9. _____

5. _____   10. _____

Report from Planet Earth

"I've finished my mapping of this planet," Glorp told the main computer in his spaceship. "I'll be heading home soon. These people are no threat to us Zingi yet. They have only just begun to travel in space. In fact, only two countries have put people into space. And only one has sent people as far as their moon. I've limited my report to that country."

1. "Their main spaceport is in the far southeast section of their country. It's actually on an island in the Atlantic Ocean. The place is called Cape Canaveral. I'll tell you its location in relation to the mainland: It's about 50 miles east of a large city called Orlando, and 18 miles southeast of the town of _____ .'"

2. "Their command center is called NASA. It's in a very large city called _____ . It's about 875 miles west of the spaceport. To get there, you have to cross the Gulf of Mexico, a large body of water. Then you cross a smaller body of water called Galveston Bay."

3. "I went about 625 miles northeast of the command center to a place called 'Rocket City, USA.' It's real name is _____ . Do you copy? It starts with the letter 'H' and has 10 letters in its name. This is where they designed the rockets that took them to the moon. There's also a camp here where children can learn about space and space science. It's 10 miles north of the Tennessee River, and 20 miles south of the border of the state of Tennessee."

4. "One of our early reports from Earth was about a man named Robert Goddard. He was one of this planet's first rocket scientists. I checked out the place where he did his work. It's in the northeastern part of this country. It's about 40 miles west and a little south of Boston, and about 25 miles northwest of Woonsocket, Rhode Island. The name of the town is _____ , but the people there pronounce it 'Wooster.'"

5. "If you travel about 340 miles southwest from there, you will come to a large city on the Potomac River. It's about 40 miles southwest of Baltimore, and it's called _____ . Here you'll find their National Air and Space Museum. It's an interesting place. But once you see it, you know that they're a long way from traveling to the stars."

6. "I flew west and a little bit north, about 400 miles. There's a town here called Wapakoneta. There's an air and space museum here, too. That's because it's the hometown of Neil Armstrong, the first person to walk on Earth's moon. The nearest city is _____ , about 15 miles north and a little east. Sounds more like a bean than a city."

7. "Next, I checked out Edwards Air Force Base. That's their number-two spaceport and the place where they test a lot of their equipment. It's far to the southwest, not far from the planet's largest ocean. The nearest large town is _____ . It's only about 10 miles south of the base, seven miles north of Palmdale, and about 50 miles north of a place called Los Angeles."

8. "I next went northwest, about 280 miles. This is an area they call 'Silicon Valley.' It's the center of their computer industry, and you can't have space travel without computers. The biggest city in the region is called _____ . It's just southeast of the southern tip of San Francisco Bay."

9. "Then I flew almost 600 miles to the east and south. On a mountain near _____ is Lowell Observatory. This is where the most distant planet from their sun was discovered. It's called Pluto—the planet, not the city. The city is about 130 miles north and a little east of Phoenix and about 80 miles south of the Grand Canyon. The city's name starts with the letter 'F.'"

10. "Before I rejoined the mother ship, I had to check out _____. Did you get that? The name has seven letters, beginning with the letter 'R.' It's about 425 miles east and south of the observatory. It's a town west of the Pecos River, about 40 miles north of Artesia. Some Earth people claim that an alien spaceship crashed here once. I don't know whether it's true. But if it is, it wasn't one of ours.

    "That's all. I'll be home in about 623 years!"

Can you identify the places Glorp mentioned in his report? Write the names of the cities and their states on the lines below.

1. _____   6. _____

2. _____   7. _____

3. _____   8. _____

4. _____   9. _____

5. _____   10. _____

Geography By the Numbers

There's nothing tricky about this activity. All you have to do is locate places on a map by latitude and longitude. Each clue is rounded to the nearest whole degree and should help you identify the exact place name. And, if you're paying attention, you should pick up another set of clues as you go along!

1. This town has the name of a snake. It's actually named after a mining company. It's located right in the middle of one of the world's greatest copper deposits, near 46° north latitude, 113° west longitude.

2. This town sounds like a place for a sport played with a ball. In fact, it is named for such a place near the original town center. We think of this sport as one played indoors, but the name of this town suggests that people once played it outdoors. The town is located at 37° north latitude, between 86° and 87° west longitude.

3. Although today you couldn't really call it a town, about 900 years ago this place was densely populated. The steep-sided canyons here were a home of the Anasazi. These Native American people dug their homes out of the cliffs or built them on ledges. We don't know what these people called themselves. Anasazi is a Navajo word meaning "they who have gone." Some Navajo have themselves built homes in these canyons, located at 36° north latitude and between 109° and 110° west longitude. By the way, the last part of its name is pronounced "shay."

4. Quick! Name a famous frontier town of the "Wild West." You may have just named this town. Around 1880, it was the world's biggest cattle market. Wyatt Earp and Bat Masterson enforced the law here. Many western gunmen lie in the town's famous "Boot Hill" cemetery, buried with their boots on. You'll find it near 38° north latitude, 100° west longitude.

5. This town is one of the coldest places in the United States. In winter, it sometimes posts the country's lowest temperature, excluding Alaska. In summer, it's the gateway to a beautiful wilderness area enjoyed by thousands of hikers and canoers—not to mention moose, bear, and other wildlife. Naturally, this city (which has only three letters in its name) is located pretty far north—near 48° north latitude and 92° west longitude.

6. This is a rather cold spot, too. It's a city of modern office buildings and old-fashioned log cabins. It's the second-largest city in its state, mainly because of the gold that's mined nearby. The best time to visit may be in late June, when this city enjoys about 22 hours of daylight! You'll find it near 64° north latitude, 148° west longitude.

7. This town was a frontier trading port in 1764. It's still a big trading port, handling lumber, paper, machinery, and dairy products. It's also the smallest city in the United States to have a major professional sports team, the team that won the first two Super Bowl games. You'll find it between 44° and 45° north latitude and at 88° west longitude.

8. This city is on an island. In fact, it's the largest city on the island. It's a port city from which beautiful tropical flowers are shipped around the world. It may have first been settled in the 800s A.D. by people from islands in the South Pacific, but it has never grown very large. That may be because of the often-active volcano to the southwest. It's between 19° and 20° north latitude, 155° west longitude.

9. This is also an island, but with very different weather. It's not a city, but it is part of a national park. You won't see any cars on the island because cars are not allowed, but you can see plenty of moose and beaver. It is part of one state, but is actually closer to another, and closer still to Canada. You'll find it at 48° north latitude and 89° west longitude.

10. This city is named for a president, who, as an army officer, fought some battles nearby. It's the largest city in population in its state and the second largest in area in the United States. You'll find it just north of 30° north latitude, and just east of 82° west longitude.

Did you find all the places suggested by the clues? Write the names of these places and the states they are located in on the lines below.

1. _____   6. _____

2. _____   7. _____

3. _____   8. _____

4. _____   9. _____

5. _____   10. _____

Where to Film the Movie

"Look, it's a very simple job," said Sid Sinnema. "It shouldn't take too long. We're looking for a place to shoot our next movie. It's a new version of Laura Ingalls Wilder's *Little Town on the Prairie*. When you've found the right place, give me a call."

"Okay, chief," replied Max Gofer. "I'll leave for the airport right away."

1. "Hello, Sid!" Max said over the phone. "I think I've got it."

    "You sound like you're shivering," Sid interrupted.

    "I am," said Max. "I'm in Alaska. The town I'm in is on the Arctic Ocean. It's the northernmost town in the United States."

    "That would be perfect—*if* we were filming Jean Craighead George's *Julie of the Wolves*," Sid said. "You must be in _____ ."

2. "Hello, Sid!" It was two days later. "How about this one? I'm in Oregon, where the Willamette River meets the Columbia. It's a beautiful city. They're having a rose festival next month."

    "I don't want cities—or roses!" Sid roared. "You must be in _____ . That's where all of Beverly Cleary's *Ramona* books are set!"

3. "Hello, Sid!" Max said excitedly. "I know you don't want cities, but this one's *historical*. A lot of the buildings date back to the 1700s, and some to the 1600s! It's in Massachusetts, on the Atlantic Ocean, just south of the mouth of the Charles River."

    "Great," Sid snarled, "but we're not making Esther Forbes's *Johnny Tremain!* Don't you know you're in _____ ?"

4. Max called back later that afternoon. "I'm in a little town, very picturesque. It's just 15 miles northwest of the last place I called you from. It's a little west of Lexington. Take down this name. Here, I'll spell it for you. C-O—"

    "Stop!" Sid roared. "You're in _____ ! That's where Louisa May Alcott grew up. We're *not* making yet another film of *Little Women!*"

5. "Okay, I'm still in Massachusetts," Max reported that evening. "I'm on the Connecticut River, just a few miles north of the state of Connecticut. It's the state's second-largest city, but it's—"

    "—The hometown of Dr. Seuss," Sid sighed. "Remember *And to Think That I Saw It on Mulberry Street?* His 'Mulberry Street' is right there, in _____ . Try again."

6. "Here's a perfect little town," Max said the next time he called. "I'm in the middle of New Hampshire, on the western edge of Lake Winnipesaukee. "Another very pretty town—"

    "—And the setting for Joan Blos's *A Gathering of Days,*" Sid interrupted. "Let me guess. Eight letters, starting with the letter 'M'?"

    "How did you know that?" asked a surprised Max.

    "Look around you, Max. You see any prairie? We want prairie! Not _____ , New Hampshire."

7. "Okay, this will do for prairie," Max called in. "I'm in _____ , Ohio. It's northeast of Dayton and southwest of Springfield. The name of the place suggests that some strangely colored water comes up out of the ground here. The writer Virginia Hamilton comes from this town."

    "And I'm sure it would do if we were filming one of her books, such as *M. C. Higgins the Great,*" sighed Sid. "But we're not. Go west, Max. West!"

8. "This is it, Sid!" Max said. "Rolling prairie and the Mississippi River. I'm in _____ , Missouri, about 100 miles northwest of St. Louis, and 20 miles south of Quincy, Illinois."

   "You're getting warmer, Max," said Sid, "but that's Mark Twain's hometown. Everyone thinks of it in connection with *The Adventures of Tom Sawyer.* Try again!"

9. "I'm not giving up, Chief!" said Max. "I'm in a town in Carbon County, Wyoming—the county seat, in fact. It's cowboy country. There are a lot of cattle ranches around here."

   "You're really close, Max!" said Sid. "If we were filming Mary O'Hara's *My Friend Flicka,* _____ would be just the right spot. Try going northeast this time."

10. "All right, now I'm in _____ , South Dakota," said a tired Max. "I'm about 35 miles east of Huron and 35 miles west of Brookings. It's the very town where Laura Ingalls Wilder grew up. There's even a *Little Town on the Prairie* monument here."

    "Great!" said Sid. "It sure took you long enough to find it!"

    "Yes," Max replied under his breath, "but I sure racked up a lot of frequent-flyer miles by pretending I didn't know where it was."

What "little towns" and big cities did Max visit? Write their names on the lines below.

1. _____   6. _____

2. _____   7. _____

3. _____   8. _____

4. _____   9. _____

5. _____   10. _____

In Search of the Perfect Meal

Congratulations! You've won first prize in the "Why I Like to Eat" essay contest. Your award is a free tour of places in the United States that are famous for food. Can you identify them from the clues below?

1. We start out with a classic American meal—beef barbecue. Of course, Texas is famous for its barbecue, but this city's is second to none. This city is located some distance north of Texas on the border of two states. You can find it at the joining place of two rivers with the same names as the states. It's about 200 miles south and west of Des Moines, Iowa, but it isn't in Iowa.

2. Take some hulled corn. Soak it in a weak lye solution until the skins come loose. Wash, cook, and grind the kernels. You've just made grits, a favorite food in the South for hundreds of years. You're eating some in a town in Mississippi. It's on the Sunflower River. It's about 25 miles west and a little south of Greenwood and the same distance east and a little north of Greenville. It's the hometown of blues musician B. B. King, and sounds like it was named for a Native American community.

3. How about some seafood next—a real New England clambake? You go to the smallest state by area in the United States to a city at the southern end of an island with the same name as the state. It's only about 25 miles from the state capital—if you go by boat. Enjoy the clams baked in a driftwood fire. Have some fish chowder and corn on the cob, too!

4. Next, you'll go to the only New England state that does not have a seacoast. The treat here is a pancake breakfast with maple syrup. You're in the heart of maple country, in the northwest corner of the state, near Lake Champlain. The maple syrup and candy made from trees near here is shipped all over the world. Burlington is about 25 miles to the south, and the Canadian border is 15 miles north of this city, the seat of Franklin County.

5. Next, try a middle-eastern feast. At this meal you'll find hummus, tabouleh, falafel, pita bread, and lots of lamb dishes. You're in a large city with a sizeable Arab population. It's on a river with the same name as the city, between Lake Erie and Lake St. Clair. From where you'll be, you can look *south* and see Canada.

6. Bread, pasta, cereal, crackers—you're in wheat country now. You're in the largest city in the greatest wheat-growing state. This city, a shipping center for wheat, is located about 130 miles southwest of Topeka, the state capital. Look around; you may get the feeling you're not in Oz any more.

7. Your next stop takes you northwest. You're in the state between Oregon and Wyoming. The town is the biggest population center on the Snake River between Boise and Pocatello. This is the heart of potato country. Would you like yours mashed, baked, scalloped, french-fried, oven-browned, or all of the above?

8. It's seafood time again. You're eating a delicious fish called mahi-mahi. You're on an island, in the southernmost state capital in the United States. Many people of Asian descent live in this state, so if you'd prefer Chinese, Japanese, or Filipino food, you're in luck.

9. Next, you fly back to the mainland. You're treated to a Mexican feast. In fact, you're only 10 miles from the Mexican border, in a city by the sea known for its navy base and its zoo. So enjoy a tamale, an enchilada, some beans and rice, and don't forget the *pollo en mole*. That's chicken in a chocolate-based sauce, a real Aztec treat!

10. Your last stop is 90 miles north and a little west—to a burger stand. How fitting! This city, about 10 miles northeast of Riverside, was home to what may have been the most famous burger stand of all. It was owned by two brothers named McDonald. They were always trying to figure out how to make more servings of food in less time. Their idea caught on—and the rest is history!

Can you identify the cities and towns where you ate these meals? Write their names and the names of their states on the lines below.

1. _____   6. _____

2. _____   7. _____

3. _____   8. _____

4. _____   9. _____

5. _____   10. _____

Geographical Features

Once Upon a Mountaintop

"I don't understand why you called me in on this job," said Anne Piton. "I'm not a detective; I'm a mountain climber."

"It's a mountain climber that we need," said Police Chief Baker. "As you know, Dick Desperate died in prison last week. He had been locked up for 10 years for the Stony Point bank job. He never told anyone what he did with the money. But just before he died, a prison doctor heard him whisper, 'It's buried under a rock at the top of a mountain.'"

"But which mountain?" Anne Piton asked.

"That's what we want you to find out," said the chief. He handed Anne a piece of paper. "We have reason to believe that it's one of these."

"I'd better start climbing," said Anne, looking at the list.

1. "I'd better start at the top," Anne said. She traveled to a national park north of Anchorage, Alaska. Here she climbed the highest mountain in the United States. It's a mountain the Native Americans call Denali, but it's better known by another name. "No money here, just a lot of snow," Anne reported back.

2. Anne next reported in from the island of Hawaii. "I'm not going near this mountain," she said. "There's no way Dick Desperate hid anything up there. It's less than 5,000 feet high, but it's a volcano—and it's erupting!"

3. After a long plane flight to Boston, Anne drove about 140 miles north and a little west to climb the highest mountain in the New England states. "It's not up there," she phoned in. "I almost got blown right off the mountain. Did you know that's the windiest place in the United States?"

4. Anne's next climb took her about 20 miles northeast of Asheville, North Carolina. "This is the highest mountain in the eastern states," she thought. "That's where I'd go if I had something to hide. But then again, all the really high mountains are in the West."

5. "I'm getting quite a workout," Anne puffed as she climbed her next mountain. It was in Wyoming's Wind River range. The mountain was 13,730 feet tall and named after a famous explorer who later ran for president. But Anne found no stolen money there.

6. In the Front Range of the Rockies, 10 miles west of Colorado Springs, Anne climbed one of the most famous mountains in the United States. "The man it's named for never even climbed it," Anne complained. "But now, they have a race here every year. People *run* to the top and run back down! No one would notice a crook in the crowd. There's no money here, however."

7. "This isn't a mountain at all," Anne said. She was near Keystone, South Dakota, looking up at her next goal. "It's really just a cliff. I don't believe Dick Desperate hid anything up here; there are always too many people looking at the presidents' faces carved into the cliff."

8. "This used to be the highest point in the United States," Anne thought. She was on a peak in California. "That was before 1959, when Alaska became a state. About 50 miles east of here, over the next mountain range, is Death Valley. That's the *lowest* point in the United States. I'm beginning to wish Dick Desperate liked low places instead of high ones."

9. Anne stood on a mountaintop about 40 miles east of Longview, Washington. "I'm sure glad I wasn't up here on May 18, 1980," she thought. "That was when this volcano last erupted. The top of the mountain was blown off, leaving it nearly a quarter-mile shorter than it had been! Dick would probably consider this too risky a place to stash the cash."

10. Anne was about to give up. The next mountain on her list was in Louisiana. "How can they call this a mountain?" she said. "It may be the highest point in this state, but it's only 535 feet high!" But wouldn't you know, that was where she found the money. "I guess Dick Desperate must have been lazy," she said when she claimed her reward.

Can you identify the mountains Anne climbed? Write their names on the lines below.

1. _____   6. _____

2. _____   7. _____

3. _____   8. _____

4. _____   9. _____

5. _____   10. _____

A "Cross-Country" Swim

Let's imagine that you're a champion swimmer. You've swum the English Channel. You've swum in the Olympic Games. You've swum just about everywhere there is to swim, indoors and out. So let's see how much you know about water in America. Below are clues to the locations of five lakes and five rivers. Not all of them are well-known, but they're all in the United States. Suppose you wanted to go for a swim in each of them to set a record. The swimming part would be easy, but finding the places might prove a little tricky.

1. We will start with a river that should be fairly easy to find. Early settlers described it as "a mile wide and an inch deep." It's one of the longest rivers in the world. Its sources are in the Rocky Mountains, in southwestern Montana. It runs through or alongside seven states on its way to the Mississippi, which it enters just north of St. Louis, Missouri. Dams now block its flow for most of its length, but it's still mighty mighty.

2. Now let's try a lake. It's at the edge of a desert, but it isn't used to irrigate crops. No dolphins swim in it, but Dolphin Island is located in its northwest corner. The towns nearby include Ogden, Bountiful, and Brigham City. You'll have to figure out what state it's in, but Wyoming and Idaho are nearby.

3. Our next river is a very short one—and it has a short name. It's not much more than 20 miles long, but millions of people live near its banks. From one end you can see the Statue of Liberty. Pass through to the other end and you're in Long Island Sound. The river flows entirely within one city. If you need any more clues, the river's name refers to its direction from Manhattan Island.

4. Here's a most unusual lake. It didn't exist before 1811, but it's not artificial. It was formed when a series of earthquakes struck near New Madrid, Missouri. The quakes created a loop in the Mississippi River. They separated the southwesternmost corner of Kentucky from the rest of the state and created this lake, about 20 miles west of Union City, Tennessee.

5. The name of this river means "red" in Spanish. It begins in the Rocky Mountains, in a state with the same name as the river. It runs through or next to four other states and part of Mexico. From Lake Powell to Lake Mead, a stretch of several hundred miles, no bridges cross the river.

6. The deepest lake in the United States is in the crater of a volcano. When the top of Mount Mazama collapsed about 6,600 years ago, it formed a hole inside the mountain. It gradually filled with water nearly 2,000 feet deep. You'll find it about 55 miles north and a little west of Klamath Falls, Oregon.

7. The source of this river is south of Waycross, Georgia. It flows south, through the Okeefenokee Swamp. In Florida it bends to the west, turns south again, and empties into the Gulf of Mexico near a town with the same name as the river. Stephen Foster wrote a famous song about this river, but he didn't spell its name correctly!

8. This lake lies south of Kalispell, Montana, and north of Missoula. Its name comes from a custom of the Salish Indians, who once lived in this region. The Salish would bind padded boards to their babies' heads. This gave them a distinctive appearance that the Salish believed to be a symbol of freedom. The babies of slaves captured in battle were not given this treatment.

9. This short river in Delaware flows northeast past Frederica and into Delaware Bay near the town of South Bowers. This river's name makes it sound as though violent crimes were committed on its banks! It's name actually comes from an old Dutch word that means "a small stream."

10. We will travel to the Midwest to visit our last lake. It's named after a Native American tribe, not a recreational vehicle! The towns along its shores include Oshkosh, Appleton, and Fond du Lac. It empties into a river flowing northeast, which in turn flows into a large bay in Lake Michigan.

Can you identify these rivers and lakes? Write their names on the lines below.

1. _____   6. _____

2. _____   7. _____

3. _____   8. _____

4. _____   9. _____

5. _____   10. _____

Capitals, West to East

The Ordoñez family is driving across the United States to attend the college graduation of the family's oldest daughter, Laura. After graduation, she won't be seeing her family much. Over the next few years, she will be traveling around the world. Follow the clues below to find out where the Ordoñez family is going to attend Laura's graduation.

1. The family leaves their hometown of San Francisco, California, and an hour and a half later, they drive through the state capital. It is on a river with the same name as the city. It has a famous railroad museum and an "old town" area where you can see tools and implements from the Gold Rush that helped this city to grow.

2. The Ordoñezes cross the Sierra Nevada, following the route of the first transcontinental railroad. On the other side of the mountains, they arrive in another state capital. It lies east of Lake Tahoe and a few miles south of Virginia City, an old silver-mining center that is now a ghost town. "This city was named for a famous frontier scout," Mrs. Ordoñez remarks. "The place where Laura has been going to college was named for a queen of England. Its name means "Anne's city."

3. The next day, after a long drive across the desert, the family arrives in another state capital. It is named for a nearby lake. The area was settled in the 1840s by the Mormons. The Ordoñezes stop to view the Mormon Tabernacle, famous for its choir.

4. The Ordoñezes cross the Rocky Mountains and stop in another state capital for the night. Coins are made in the United States mint in this city on the South Platte River. "This city grew up after a gold strike in 1858," Mr. Ordoñez remarks. "The place we're going was first settled long before that—in 1649."

5. The next day, the travelers follow the Platte River across the Great Plains. They feel like they are driving through a 500-mile-long corn field. They stop that night in a state capital named for a president of the United States. "I'll bet this city didn't get its name until after the Civil War," Rita says.

6. The Ordoñezes are still in corn-growing country the following day. They cross the Missouri River and pass through a city on the Raccoon River. "The name of this city sounds French," Rita remarks. "The French explorers must have traded in this area a long time ago."

   "And it's *another* state capital," Paul adds. "Isn't the place Laura lives a capital, too?"

   "Yes," his mother answers. "In fact, it has the oldest state capitol building still in use."

7. The family turns southeast and crosses the Mississippi River. That evening the Ordoñezes stay in yet another state capital. They tour Abraham Lincoln's home and the office where he practiced law. "I would have guessed that Chicago was the capital of this state," Paul says. "This city seems too small to be a capital."

8. The next day, the Ordoñezes drive southwest across another state and across the Ohio River. They drive through another small capital, in an area famous for the breeding of horses. About 25 miles further to the southeast, they pass through the city of Lexington.

9. The Ordoñezes are in sight of the Ohio River again when they drive east into another state. They spend the night in its capital, where the Elk and New rivers come out of the Allegheny Mountains to form the Kanawha. "We should get there tomorrow," Mrs. Ordoñez says. "Just one more state to go."

   "Great!" says Rita. "I can't wait to see Laura, and to tour the United States Naval Academy."

10. The family watches Laura graduate in a stirring ceremony. Nearby, the Severn River empties into Chesapeake Bay. "I'm glad we're here. It was a long trip, but it was a fun trip, too" Rita says.

    "You might even say it was a *capital* trip," Paul adds.

Can you name the capitals and states that the Ordoñez family visited? Write them on the lines below.

1. _____   6. _____

2. _____   7. _____

3. _____   8. _____

4. _____   9. _____

5. _____   10. _____

From the Mountains to the Prairies

You've heard of the Rocky Mountains and the Great Lakes. These activities have asked you to climb Pikes Peak and descend into Death Valley, to explore the mighty Mississippi and the Great Plains. But the United States is a big country. It contains many geographical features that are well known by the people who live near them, but not so well known by the rest of us. See how many of these you can identify.

1. We'll start in one of the country's largest deserts. It measures about 25,000 square miles in area, between the Colorado River and the Sierra Nevada, Tehachapi, and San Bernardino mountains. It contains a lot of dry lakes and extinct volcanoes, and is home to a unique plant known as the Joshua tree.

2. We next travel several hundred miles to the north and west to a chain of volcanoes that are not so extinct. One of them, Mount St. Helens, erupted as recently as 1980. Another, Lassen Peak, was last active in 1921. This volcanic range extends through three states and into Canada. Its highest peak is Mount Rainier, at 14,410 feet. The chain is named for the many waterfalls that tumble from its heights.

3. Cowboys of earlier days called this treeless plain a desert. They dreaded bringing cattle across it because of the lack of water. Today, thanks to irrigation, this area is a rich farming region. It lies in northwest Texas, east of the Pecos River and west of the city of Lubbock. Its Spanish name means "staked plain."

4. About 800 miles north is a heart-shaped range of mountains. It is sacred to the Dakota, or Sioux, Indians. They named it for the dark pine forests that once covered its slopes. But the Indians were driven out and the forests cut down after gold was discovered there in 1874. Harney Peak, at 7,242 feet, is the highest point of the range. Rapid City is the largest nearby town.

5. Now we go about 300 miles southeast, into another state. We're in a low range of grassy hills, between the Niobrara and North Platte rivers. Its name tells you something about the soil here. Some counties in this region have fewer than 1,000 people. But the grass that once fed millions of buffalo now nourishes great numbers of beef cattle.

6. The name of this region makes it sound as though this might not be a nice place to visit. Millions of visitors have looked beyond its name, however, and have come here to view this colorful country of rugged rock formations. It lies east of the Little Missouri River, about 125 miles west of Bismarck, a state capital. President Theodore Roosevelt once worked at a ranch in this region, which now contains a park named for him.

7. Now we come to a range of low mountains that covers parts of Oklahoma, Arkansas, and Missouri. More than 10,000 springs bubble out of the ground here. The region is full of underground streams and deep caves, and much of it is covered by forests. Springfield, Missouri, is the largest town in the area.

8. Let's go northeast now, across Illinois, and up the length of Lake Michigan. West of the Strait of Mackinac is a chain of islands. The largest one is named for an animal that makes good use of the islands' trees. People, too, live on this island. You can get there by boat from the town of Charlevoix, Michigan. Winter ice, however, often restricts the islanders to the island and visitors to the mainland.

9. We're in the East now, looking up at the Appalachian Mountains. The chain's eastern ranges have a distinctive hue. Of course, they're not really that color when you get up close, but now you know how they got their name. The mountains cover parts of six states, from Pennsylvania to Georgia. Mount Mitchell in North Carolina is the tallest peak east of the Mississippi, at 6,684 feet.

10. We started this journey in a desert. Let's end it in a swamp. It covers about 700 square miles, about 60 miles east of Valdosta in one southeastern state and 80 miles north of Gainesville in another. Today, most of it is a national wildlife refuge. In earlier times, it was used as a refuge by runaway slaves.

Identify the geographical locations described in the clues and write their names on the lines below.

1. _____   6. _____

2. _____   7. _____

3. _____   8. _____

4. _____   9. _____

5. _____   10. _____

General Mysteries

Sidewinder Sue's Lost Treasure

While browsing in a library, you find a letter hidden inside an old book. It was written by none other than Susan Hinch, known from legend as "Sidewinder Sue." Sue claimed to have found a fabulous gold mine in California. No one ever believed her story. But in her letter, Sue tells of a map showing the location of the mine. She divided the map in nine pieces and hid each of them in a different town or city in California. Use the clues below to identify the places Sue hid the map pieces. Once you've pieced together the map, use the last clue to find the gold mine.

1. The first piece of the map is found in a desert outpost, near the ghost town of Calico. It is about 110 miles south of the town of Death Valley Junction and 150 miles west of the Arizona state line. It's the largest city on the Mojave River, which is dry most of the year. It was once a gathering place for miners.

2. From there, travel about 155 miles south to the state's second-largest city to find the next piece of the map. It's on the ocean, just north of the Mexican border. The Spanish first arrived in its fine harbor in 1542. The city has a large naval base and is a center for the airplane-building industry, but it may be most famous for its zoo.

3. You'll find the next piece of the map in a city about 110 miles northwest. It's the state's largest city, and the second-largest city in the United States. It was founded by Spanish settlers in 1781. It is known by a short form of its Spanish name, which means "The town of Our Lady, Queen of the Angels." Today, it's the center of the entertainment industry, which is usually identified with one small part of the city—Hollywood.

4. To find the fourth piece, follow the Pacific coast west and north for about 100 miles. The Spanish priest Junipero Serra set up a chain of 21 missions in California in the 1700s. The mission in this city is one of the best preserved, but the city is mostly known for its beaches, which draw visitors from all over the world. You'll see Santa Cruz Island if you look south across the Pacific Ocean from this city with two words in its name.

5. Travel due north from here across the mountains for 170 miles and you'll come to the city where you'll find the next piece of the map. In Sue's day, it was just a small farming community. Today it's a major city in California's San Joaquin Valley, one of America's richest food-producing regions.

6. Now go 125 miles west and a little south. Sue hid another piece of the map in this town, which is located on a bay of the same name. It was California's capital until 1850, under Spanish, Mexican, and American rule. Today, however, it's mainly known for its aquarium.

7. To find the next piece of the map you will need to travel northwest along the coast for about 90 miles. You come to the city where Sidewinder Sue and other gold hunters used to come for their weekend fun. It's still a favorite city of tourists. A hundred years ago, it was California's largest city and main business center. Today, most of its shipping business has been lost to Oakland, across the bay. San Jose, about 60 miles southeast, has more people, but this city is still the "capital" of this part of California.

8. About 65 miles east is where Sue hid the next piece of the map. The city is in California's central valley, but it's a port for ocean-going ships. The San Joaquin River and a system of canals link it with San Francisco Bay. It is a county seat about 50 miles south and a little east of Sacramento, the state capital.

9. It's about 250 miles northwest "as the crow flies" to the last piece of the map, but the trip is worth it. "I have found it!" you exclaim, as you put the pieces together. Indeed, that is exactly what the name of this town means! It's another county seat and an old lumber-milling center, located across a bay from Arcata and about 100 miles west and a little north of Redding.

10. You put the map together. Now you know where Sidewinder Sue's lost mine is! You go southeast, through Red Bluff, Chico, Oroville, and Marysville. Then you cut east, toward the towering Sierra Nevada, until you come to Grass Valley. Sue's mine is in a small town just five miles further northeast. The name of the town makes it sound as though it belongs in the next state east. Parts of the town do date back to Gold Rush times. But don't stop here; you've still got a lot of digging to do!

Can you name all the cities and towns where Sue hid the pieces of her map? Can you name the town where her gold mine is located? Write their names on the lines below.

1. _____   6. _____

2. _____   7. _____

3. _____   8. _____

4. _____   9. _____

5. _____   10. _____

On the Trail of Lightfingers Louie

My name is Frank. I'm a detective. I'll never forget the time I was after Lightfingers Louie. He had stolen a valuable painting from an art museum. I knew he had it in the trunk of his car. I could have caught him red-handed, but I suspected that there were even bigger crooks behind the job. I figured that if I followed Louie, he would lead me right to them.

1. I spotted Louie eating lobster for breakfast in a restaurant by a rocky seashore. We were in "the pine tree state," but I didn't see any pine trees. It's the only state that borders on just one other state.

2. I followed Louie as he drove southwest through several states. We passed through the cities of Boston, Providence, and New Haven. Louie never suspected that I was following him. But soon after we crossed into the next state, I almost lost him in a traffic jam. The state we were in is home to the nation's largest city. The city and the state share the same name.

3. We went through several more large cities, including the capital of the United States. We crossed the Potomac River. If it had been a clear day, I might have been able to see the Blue Ridge Mountains far to the west. About an hour later, during which we crossed no more state lines, Louie stopped for the night at a motel looking out on Chesapeake Bay.

4. The next morning, Louie drove south. I followed him into the next state. It's the only eastern state that does not have a river's path forming any part of its borders.

5. Here, Louie turned west. That afternoon, we crossed several mountain ranges in the Appalachians, passed through a national park, and came down into flat land again. We stopped here for the night. We were in another state; it's one of two states that border eight other states.

6. Three days had passed, and Louie still didn't realize anyone was following him! That evening, we crossed the Mississippi River. Now we were in the other state that borders eight states.

7. I had a feeling that the case was about to break. Surely Louie was not coming all this way for nothing. But he kept on going. Late that night, we crossed the Missouri River into yet another state. Louie stopped here for the night. The city we were in had the same name as the city on the other side of the river in the state we had just left!

8. Wherever Louie was making the drop, it lay further west. We drove almost due west for hours the next day, through what seemed to be one huge field of wheat. That evening found us in another state. Here Louie made a few phone calls. We had been crossing the Great Plains, but the ground had been rising higher and higher all day. I could see the Rocky Mountains from my motel window.

9. We did not cross the Rockies that day, but could see them on the right as we drove, crossing another state border. Finally we turned west and drove up the Sangre de Cristo Range of the Rockies. That evening found us in another state capital, the oldest capital in the United States. It has been a seat of government since 1610.

10. Louie drove on through the night, and I followed. We continued west and crossed a river whose name means "big river" in Spanish. We crossed mountains and a desert, into another state. In Petrified Forest National Park, Louie pulled into a parking lot. Here I caught him trying to sell the painting to Maurice de Fens, the notorious art smuggler!

   I had a $25,000 reward coming to me!

Can you identify the states suggested by the clues? Write their names on the lines below.

1. _____   6. _____

2. _____   7. _____

3. _____   8. _____

4. _____   9. _____

5. _____   10. _____

The Stolen Wedding Ring

"Let me get this straight," said Detective Pam Quest. "You *think* your brother-in-law Mack has run off with your mother's wedding ring? And you *think* he's hiding out in a city in this state?" Her fingertips did a drumroll on the map on her desk.

"I know it's a big state," said Lucy, tearfully. "There are a lot of wide-open spaces to hide in. But Mack wouldn't hide out in ranch country. He likes cities. And it would mean so much to me to get that ring back."

"All right," Pam Quest sighed. "I'll take the case. Let me have that picture of your brother-in-law. I'll see what I can do. I'd better get my pickup truck fixed first; I'll be doing a lot of driving."

1. Lucy is right—it *is* a big state. In area, it is the second-largest state in the United States! It measures 800 miles from New Mexico on its western border to Louisiana on its eastern border, and another 800 miles from north to south.

2. That very afternoon, Pam leaves her hometown. Its name is Spanish for "the pass." It lies in a gap between the Franklin Mountains and the Sierra Madre, just across the Rio Grande from Ciudad Juarez, Mexico. (Before 1848, the two cities were one.)

3. Pam drives due east about 240 miles. She comes to a city that is a center for oil drilling, about 20 miles southwest of Midland. Mack has worked in the oil business, but no one Pam meets in the town recognizes his picture. "This town must have been settled by Ukrainian immigrants," Pam thinks." It has the same name as a city in Ukraine."

4. The next morning, Pam drives about 125 miles north and a little east. She looks for Mack in a city on the high plains along a fork of the Brazos River. The town is in the middle of cotton-growing country and is a leading processor of cotton. Its name has seven letters, beginning with the letter "L." Pam finds no trace of the jewel thief here.

5. Pam continues north, about 115 miles, into an area of the state called "the Panhandle." She comes to the area's largest city, whose name is Spanish for "yellow." It's a center for the cattle and oil industries. Northeast of town is a factory where nuclear weapons are made. "Speaking of which, I'm sure 'bombing out' on this search," Pam says to herself. "Maybe I'd better try another direction."

6. The next day, Pam drives a little more than 400 miles southeast to a city on the Colorado River. She spends a day looking through the state police's file of known crooks. She also checks out other government agencies. The city she is in is named for two pioneers in this state who were father and son. Pam passes the evening enjoying a rock concert near the state university.

7. Following a lead from the state police, Pam heads 70 miles southwest. She looks for Mack in one of the oldest cities in the state. It's also one of the most modern and fastest growing, with many hospitals and medical research centers. Pam shows Mack's picture around River Walk, a pretty shopping area along a river with the same name as the city. No one recognizes him.

8. The next day, Pam drives 225 miles east to a seaport city. It lies on a bay with the same name as the city, about 45 miles southeast of Houston, the state's largest city. A worker at an offshore oil well recognizes Mack's picture! "He was here earlier this week," he informs Pam. "I think he said he was heading north."

9. Pam heads north and then turns west. She passes through Dallas and drives 30 miles further. She comes to an industrial city that is home to a famous children's museum. She checks out the offices of the many oil companies in town. In one, she picks up Mack's trail. "He tried to sell me that ring," a woman tells her. "I wouldn't buy it— I thought he looked shifty. He said he was heading east, maybe out of state."

10. In the northeastern corner of the state, Pam finally catches up with Mack. She spots him in a town on the border with another state. Its name combines the names of both states.

    Soon Mack is on his way to jail—and Pam Quest begins the long drive back home to return the ring to Lucy.

Can you identify the state where the story takes place, the city Pam started from, and all the places she stopped? Write their names on the lines below.

1. _____   6. _____

2. _____   7. _____

3. _____   8. _____

4. _____   9. _____

5. _____   10. _____

The Empire State Caper

I was in the Empire State. In fact, I was at the top of the Empire State Building. I was in the largest city in the United States, trying to see as far as I could see. That was because of Jack, a rich friend of mine who likes to play pranks. He told me he had $10,000 for me in a safe-deposit box at a bank. To get the key, though, I had to meet him that Friday afternoon at three o'clock, on a ship called *The Maid of the Mist*. From where I was standing, I could see a lot of water and a lot of ships.

1. I was looking south, across a busy river, to another borough of this huge city. I went there first. The place was originally called "Breuckelen," after a village in Holland. I looked at every ship in port, but couldn't find the one I was looking for.

2. I crossed the Verrazano-Narrows Bridge to yet another borough of the same city. It was actually an island. Where there was an island there should be ships, right? Wrong! At least, the ship I was looking for wasn't there. The borough didn't seem like it belonged in the same city—or even the same state, for that matter. It's actually closer to New Jersey.

3. I traveled about 160 miles north, up the Hudson River to the state capital. All the length of the river, I was looking for the *Maid of the Mist*, but I didn't even see any mist. I saw a lot of boats—river boats, canal boats, even ocean-going ships—but not the one I wanted.

4. A few miles further north, I came to a city that is across the Hudson from the town of Watervliet. It's an old city, and it was named for a *really* old one. I didn't find my ship there, but I did find out that the city was once the home of Uncle Sam. ("Uncle Sam," of course, is a symbol of the United States government, but the name is said to have come from "Uncle" Sam Wilson, who supplied food to the army from this city in 1812.)

5. Next, I tried a lake. It was just north of a town with the same name as the lake. It's a pretty town in the northeastern part of the state, about 10 miles southeast of Saranac Lake. Twice the Winter Olympic Games have been held here. I saw two big islands in the lake, and a lot of boats, but not the ship I was looking for.

6. I decided to try a bigger lake. I went to Oneida Lake and, from there, about 25 miles northwest to a city on one of the Great Lakes. It's the easternmost port on the Great Lakes, in fact. The name of the city is an anagram of "gwoose," but it's sometimes called "snow city" because of the heavy winters here. Plenty of snow, maybe, but no mist and no *Maid*.

7. About 35 miles southeast of there is Onondaga Lake. A big manufacturing city is located on its shores. Before 1825, it was only a small village where Native Americans and European settlers produced salt from nearby springs. Then the Erie Canal was built through here, and later a railroad, and the place became a major factory town and center of trade. I saw plenty of canal barges, but not one of them would have qualified as a ship.

8. I was at my wits' end. I traveled about 45 miles southwest, to do some research at Cornell University. It stands in a town at the southern end of Cayuga Lake. I didn't find my ship in the lake, but I did find it in a book describing the state's tourist attractions. What a fool I had been! I jumped in my car and headed west.

9. Time was running out. Wouldn't you know, I got stuck in traffic in the state's second-largest city! The city, which is named for an animal, is located at the far eastern end of Lake Erie. "Come on," I urged the cars in front of me. I had just miles to go!

10. It was only about 20 miles, in fact, to the north and west. I could see the mist before I got there and I could hear the roar of the falling water that caused the mist. In the town named for the waterfall, I got directions to the *Maid of the Mist*. The boat was just pulling away from the dock for its cruise below the thundering falls. There was Jack, looking out over the rail. "Thought you'd never make it, old boy," he said casually, as he handed me the key to the $10,000.

Can you name all the boroughs, cities, and towns where Jack's friend searched? Write their names on the lines below.

1. _____   6. _____

2. _____   7. _____

3. _____   8. _____

4. _____   9. _____

5. _____   10. _____

Just For Fun

Inventions, East to West

This puzzler asks you to identify places associated with various inventions. Some of the clues may stretch your understanding of what the word "invention" means. You'll find the "birthplaces" of technological inventions, such as the telephone and television; but you'll also visit the hometowns of a tasty treat, an article of clothing, a popular art form, a famous song, and a type of music. Your search for these inventions will take you across the United States, starting in the northeast.

1. You will begin in a New England city that was a center for American ideas and the arts throughout the 1800s. You will find this city in Suffolk County, Massachusetts. Among the items invented here were the *sewing machine* (by Elias Howe, in 1846) and the *telephone* (by Alexander Graham Bell, in 1876).

2. Now go about 220 miles southwest to a large city. It is bounded by the Hudson River, Long Island Sound, Raritan Bay, and another bay with the same name as the city. Here, in 1895, a newspaper cartoonist named Richard Outcault drew the first *comic strip.* It was called "Hogan's Alley," and it first appeared in a newspaper called *The World.*

3. Continue southwest another hundred miles. Where the Schuylkill River meets the Delaware, you'll come to another large city. Here, in 1883, Charles Stillwell invented something that nobody gives much thought. Yet Americans use more than 40 billion of them every year. He called it the "S.O.S.," which stood for "self-opening sack." We know it as the simple, lowly, flat-bottomed, pleat-sided *brown paper bag*.

4. Now go about 400 miles west and a little north to a city on the Cayahoga River, where it empties into Lake Erie. *Rock-and-roll* music was not invented here. But it was in this city, in 1951, that a radio "disk jockey" named Alan Freed may first have used that name to describe what was then a new style of music. For this reason, the Rock and Roll Hall of Fame and Museum is located here.

5. Speaking of music, go to the southwest corner of the state you are in. Cross the river named for the state, into another state. Then go about 85 miles southwest to that state's largest city. Here, in 1893, two sisters named Mildred and Patty Hill wrote a song called "Good Morning to All." Later, with different words, it became the most frequently sung song in the world! It has been translated into hundreds of languages. In English, we know it as *"Happy Birthday to You."*

6. Continue southwest along the river until you reach Paducah. Then cross the river into another state. Go 160 miles north and a little west, into Shelby County. Here, in the county seat, a rich woman named Josephine Cochrane became frustrated that her expensive plates were continually being broken as they were washed by her household staff. In 1886, she set to work building a machine that would do the job. Her *automatic dishwasher* was an immediate hit with hotels and restaurants, but it was not until later that the device caught on in private homes.

7. Now go due north about 170 miles. You'll come to a town (with the same name as its county) on the Kishwaukee River, about 60 miles due west of Chicago. Here is where Joseph Glidden, in 1874, introduced the invention that transformed the West. It allowed small farmers to fence in land. In this way, *barbed wire* made possible the settlement of the frontier.

8. Go south and west, to the place where the Illinois River meets the Mississippi. Cross the Mississippi and go about 30 miles southeast to a big city. During a world's fair held here in 1904, a teenager named Arnold Fornachou was running an ice-cream stand. One day, he ran out of paper serving dishes. At a neighboring stand, a Syrian immigrant named Ernest Hamwi was selling waffles. Thinking quickly, Fornachou rolled one of Hamwi's waffles into a cone. His invention, the *ice cream cone*, was reported in newspapers the next day.

9. No one person invented television, but one of the most important inventions that led to TV—the *image dissector*—came from the workshop of Philo Farnsworth. This happened when Farnsworth was only 16 years old! He lived in a small town and county named for an animal. It lies about 125 miles north of the Grand Canyon and about 25 miles southeast of the town of Milford.

10. In this West Coast city in 1872, a German immigrant named Levi Strauss owned a dry-goods business. A tailor suggested to him that he use metal rivets to strengthen the seams of work pants. Two years later, the first *blue jeans* came off Strauss's sewing machines. They quickly became known as "Levis," the name by which they are still called today. Levi Strauss's original factory still stands in this city, about 90 miles southwest of Sacramento and just a few miles west of Oakland.

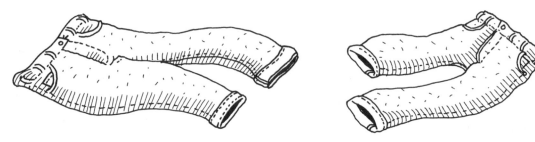

Can you identify the cities and towns associated with these inventions? Write their names on the lines below.

1. _____   6. _____

2. _____   7. _____

3. _____   8. _____

4. _____   9. _____

5. _____   10. _____

In the Wilderness

"Yes, that's her, all right." said Adam Truehart, park ranger, as FBI Agent Kimura set the photograph down in front of him. "Laura Lamont—the notorious fur- and feather-poacher. Endangered species are her specialty; there's not an ocelot or bald eagle safe if Lamont's on the loose."

Adam stared angrily at the photo. "And to think she's disguised herself as a park ranger. Our job is to *protect* wildlife. People trust us."

"Then you'll find her for us?" Kimura asked.

"I'll do my best, sir," Adam said. "But all you've told me is that she's working in a national park. There are a lot of them."

"You can use one of our helicopters," said the FBI officer.

1. Adam started his search at one of the most beautiful and most popular of all national parks. It was in the mountains east of the city of Stockton, California. "I'd like to stay and climb Half Dome," he said, looking out over the beautiful valley, "but I can't stop now." A ranger recognized Lamont's photograph. "Yes, she was here," she said. "I think it was too dry for her. I heard her say she wanted to go someplace rainier."

2. Adam flew to the state of Washington. He landed at a national park southeast of the city of Seattle. Its 14,410-foot inactive volcano was visible hundreds of miles away. He learned that someone fitting Lamont's description had been there a month ago. She had left, mumbling something about ice.

3. Adam flew eastward. He landed at a park on the Canadian border in Montana, named for its more than 50 slow-moving masses of ice. "A lot of mountain goats are here," Adam muttered. "There are bighorn sheep, too. If Lamont's harmed a hair on any of their heads . . . ." Indeed, he found an illegal trap, but thankfully no animal was caught in it. Nearby he spotted a scrap of paper torn from of a map. An area was circled in the southern part of the state, where it joined two other states.

4. Adam flew south and east. His next stop was the largest of all the national parks in the "lower 48" states. It takes up parts of three states and is famous for its geysers. "And grizzly bears," Adam thought. "They're such beautiful animals." No harm had come to the bears from the cruel Ms. Lamont, but a guide recognized her picture. "I think she said something about heading southeast," the guide said. "Or was it south-west?"

5. Adam's next stop was Colorado, and a park famous for its mountains. "There are more than 100 peaks higher than 10,000 feet," Adam thought. "Lamont certainly isn't afraid of heights!" He showed her photograph to the rangers, but none had seen her. "She must have said *southwest*," he thought.

6. Adam flew west into another state. He got clearance to bring the helicopter down in a park 50 miles east of the town of Cedar City. Here there were deep valleys lined with brightly colored layers of rock. They seemed to change in color and shape as the sun moved westward. But Adam couldn't stay to watch. A tourist said she had seen someone fitting Lamont's description south of there. "She was peering down at the Colorado River," the woman said.

7. Adam went on to a national park in Arizona. He flew over the great gorge, carved by the Colorado River, that gave the park its name. Several people at the park head-quarters recognized the woman in the photo. "I thought she was a ranger!" a man said. "She said she'd seen too much desert and was going to a place where there was plenty of water."

8. Adam's next stop was one of the wettest places in the whole national parks system. He spent several days near the Canadian border in Minnesota, paddling a canoe and carrying his gear from one lake or river to another. "It's getting late in the summer," he thought. "Maybe Lamont went someplace warmer."

9. Adam flew southeast, to the most-visited national park in the United States. It straddles two states and has some of the highest mountains east of the Mississippi River. "Yes, I've spoken to her!" a ranger said excitedly when she saw Lamont's picture. "She seemed to think that this place was named for that bear—you know, the one that's a symbol of forest-fire prevention? She said something else that sounded strange coming from a park ranger. She said she'd always wanted to have an alligator purse!"

10. Alligators! Adam realized where Lamont was. He flew to the southeasternmost large city in the continental United States. From there he went due west into a great swamp famous for its subtropical wildlife. Here he found Laura Lamont, wearing her ranger's disguise and trying to capture an alligator. Adam called the FBI. "The wildlife in our national parks will sleep more easily tonight," Adam said, as he turned Laura Lamont over to the authorities.

Can you identify all of the national parks where Adam searched for Laura Lamont? Write their names on the lines below.

1. _____   6. _____

2. _____   7. _____

3. _____   8. _____

4. _____   9. _____

5. _____   10. _____

The Honored and Remembered

This adventure takes you on a mysterious journey to 10 monuments and memorials. Some of them honor American heroes, while others are monuments to ideas or historical events. One is a statue of a character in a poem. There's even one that's a tribute to an insect! See how many of their locations you can identify from the clues.

1. We start just across the Potomac River from our nation's capital—directly opposite the Lincoln Memorial, in fact. In this city, you'll find the Tomb of the Unknown Soldier. Here rest the bodies of unidentified American soldiers killed in four 20th-century wars. Many other Americans who served in our country's armed forces are buried in the national cemetery here. So are presidents William Howard Taft and John Fitzgerald Kennedy.

2. Our next stop is a monument to peace. The International Peace Garden lies near the middle of our nearly 4,000-mile-long border with Canada—a border that has seen no fighting since 1814. You'll find the International Peace Garden just north of this town, which itself is 12 miles east of the town of Bottineau.

3. Ellis Island was the place where 12 million new Americans first set foot on the shores of our country. From 1892 to 1924, it was the main United States immigration center. Today it is a monument and museum. It lies in the harbor of this large city, though it is actually closer to Jersey City, New Jersey.

4. Francis Scott Key wrote "The Star-Spangled Banner" while he was a prisoner on a the British ship that attacked Fort McHenry during the War of 1812. Today the fort is a national monument. It honors the defense of this city against the British. The city is about 40 miles northeast of Washington, D.C., and 50 miles south of York, Pennsylvania.

5. A national memorial marks the site of Abraham Lincoln's boyhood home. Visitors can see the cabin where Lincoln lived from age 7 to 21 and the grave of his mother. The memorial is located near the town of Lincoln City, about 75 miles west of Louisville, Kentucky, and less than 35 miles northeast of this large city on the northern banks of the Ohio River.

6. Architect Maya Lin designed a monument to the heroes of the movement for African-American civil rights. It stands in the city where the movement is said to have begun in 1955. It is located about 140 miles east of Meridian, Mississippi and the same distance northeast of Pensacola, Florida, but it is in neither Mississippi nor Florida.

7. In the same state, about 80 miles south and a little east of the state capital, is a monument to the boll weevil. This insect larva destroyed this state's cotton crop early in the 20th century. So why a monument? Because farmers were forced to grow different and more diverse crops and, as a result, they became more prosperous. The boll weevil monument is in the town square of this Coffee County community, whose name means "business activity."

8. Now travel westward two states. Find a town that's about 15 miles southeast of Lafayette and 45 miles southwest of Baton Rouge. (It's named after someone named Martin.) In this town stands a statue of a woman named Evangeline. She was a member of the French people known as Acadians (or "Cajuns") who were forced to leave their homes in eastern Canada and settle here in 1755. "Evangeline" may or may not have been a real person; but her legend was made secure in a poem by Henry Wadsworth Longfellow.

9. Our next stop is in a western state. The Nez Percé National Historical Park honors the culture and history of the Nez Percé people. It also honors Lewis and Clark, the first non-Indians to explore this region. It's near a town on the Snake River, about 15 miles south of Moscow and just across the river from Clarkston, Washington.

10. "Independence Rock" was a landmark on the Oregon Trail. Pioneers heading west would carve their names and messages into this huge rock on the plains of what is now Wyoming. You can still read their words if you visit Independence Rock today. It is still very much in "the middle of nowhere," about 150 miles northwest of Cheyenne and about 45 miles southwest of this city on the North Platte River.

Can you identify the sites of these monuments and memorials? Write the names of their cities and states on the lines below.

1. _____
2. _____
3. _____
4. _____
5. _____

6. _____
7. _____
8. _____
9. _____
10. _____

Mystery Locations: Sports

My name is Jock Rooter. I'm a sports fan. I'm traveling around the country visiting famous and not-so-famous places in the world of sports. At the end of my trip, I'm going to take in a big sports event that I once dreamed of playing in. See if you can guess what it is before I get there—and if you can identify the other places I stop in on the way.

1. First, I will visit a town in Montana. It's probably the *least* likely site in history for a championship sports event. Yet it was here in 1923 that Jack Dempsey beat challenger Tommy Gibbons to keep his world heavyweight boxing title. The town lies near the Canadian border, about 75 miles northwest of Great Falls. There are six letters in its name, starting with the letter "S." (The event I'm going to see will involve some hitting, but there won't be any heavyweights.)

2. Next, I'll go south to visit the "Speed Capital of the United States." Just east of this town is Utah's Bonneville Speedway. Here, drivers in rocket-powered cars keep raising the land speed record ever higher. The town lies due west of the state capital and just a mile from a state line. (I'd be really surprised if anyone participating in the event I'm going to see has ever driven a car.)

3. Too bad it's summer! Otherwise, I could attend a World Cup Ski Tournament. They hold one every year in a resort town I'll be passing through. It's high in the Rocky Mountains of Colorado, about 100 miles southwest of Denver and about 35 miles southeast of Glenwood Springs. Its name has five letters and begins with "A." (I won't see any ski runs in the event I'm going to, but I may see a few unearned runs.)

4. Now I'm in the large Nebraska city where baseball's "College World Series" is played. Fans come here every spring to see future major-league stars compete in an eight-team tournament. The city is on the Missouri River, just across from Council Bluffs, Iowa. (I'm going to be attending a "world series," but none of the players I'm going to see has ever been to college.)

5. Is there a capital of football? If fans were to name one, it might be this Indiana city where the "Fighting Irish" of Notre Dame play. It's about 75 miles east of Chicago, and it gets its name from its location at a bend in the St. Joseph River. (I hope I won't be seeing any kicking or tackling where I'm going.)

6. Next, I travel northeast to a city in Michigan. It's a county seat about 40 miles west of Detroit and 50 miles south of Flint. It was here in 1935 that Jesse Owens gave the greatest one-day performance in the history of track and field. Within 45 minutes, he broke three world records and tied a fourth! (Of course, I prefer team sports myself.)

7. Now I'm in a large city in Massachusetts. I'm near the southern edge of the state, on a river with the same name as a neighboring state. The Basketball Hall of Fame is here. James Naismith invented the game in this city in 1891. He was a college sports coach who had been asked to create a team game that could be played indoors during the winter. About 20 miles north of here is Amherst, where Julius Erving and Marcus Camby both played basketball for the University of Massachusetts. (The players I'm going to see aren't quite that tall. The ball isn't as big, either.)

8. You may or may not know that baseball was *not* first played in Cooperstown, New York in 1839. That popular story is only that—a story. The game as we know it today is actually based on rules set forth by Alexander Cartwright in 1845. The first game between organized teams took place the following summer, in a New Jersey town, across the Hudson River from New York City. The name of the town has seven letters, beginning with "H." (By now you may have figured out that it's baseball that I'm going to see, too.)

9. On August 31, 1895, a football team from this Pennsylvania town beat a team from nearby Jeannette, 12-0. This was the first professional football game ever played, 25 years before the NFL was formed. The town is about midway between Pittsburgh and Johnstown. It's also the hometown of golf great Arnold Palmer. Its name begins with an "L" and has seven letters. (By the way, the place I'm heading for is northeast of here across the state.)

10. Well, I'm finally here! I'm in a city on the Susquehanna River, about 60 miles west of Wilkes-Barre, Pennsylvania. That's my kid there at bat! Yes, indeed, I'm at the Little League World Series! Did you figure it out?

Can you identify the places Jock visited? Write the names of the cities and states on the lines below.

1. _____   6. _____

2. _____   7. _____

3. _____   8. _____

4. _____   9. _____

5. _____   10. _____

Meet Me at the Festival

For this map mystery, let's go to a party. In fact, let's go to 10 of them! Each of the places you must find is the home of a local festival. There are food festivals and music festivals, cultural festivals and sports festivals. I'm sure you'll have a good time at all of them—if you can find your way there!

1. We begin in a big West Coast city on Easter Sunday. Here, near the city's original Spanish settlement, children bring their pets to a church to be blessed. The "Blessing of the Animals" comes from an old Mexican tradition. It is very popular among the large Mexican-American population that live here. This city, which shares its Spanish name with the county, is located about 125 miles northwest of the Mexican border.

2. The rodeo is an annual event held in many western cities. It is both a contest and a demonstration of the skills of working cowboys and cowgirls. One of the most famous rodeos is held every year in this northeastern Oregon town. It's on the Umatilla River, about 30 miles southeast of where it joins the Columbia, and just west of the Umatilla Indian Reservation.

3. Most Native American peoples have their own tribal festivals. The Inter-Tribal Indian Ceremonial, however, draws Indian people from all over North America. It's held every August in a city on the Puerco River in New Mexico. The city is located about 15 miles from the Arizona border, in between the Navajo and Zuñi reservations. Its name makes it sound like the Indians' horses are hurrying to the ceremonial, too!

4. "Juneteenth" refers to June 19, 1865. This was the day that African-Americans in eastern Texas got the news of the end of the Civil War—and of their slavery. Juneteenth celebrations are held in African-American communities all over the United States, including this city in Jefferson County, Texas. It's about 20 miles northwest of Port Arthur and 25 miles west of the Louisiana border.

5. One of the most famous of all festivals is held in this Louisiana city on the Mississippi River and the southern shore of Lake Pontchartrain. *Mardi Gras* is French for "fat Tuesday," and is the name of an ancient religious holiday. But here, as in other places, it is mainly observed today with feasting, dancing, and a costume parade.

6. The great jazz musician Leon "Bix" Beiderbecke grew up in this city in Iowa. At the time of his death, in 1931, Beiderbecke was relatively unknown. But his music is remembered every July in a memorial jazz festival in his hometown. It's on the Mississippi River, right across from Rock Island and Moline, Illinois.

7. Music of a different kind is celebrated in Kentucky every September. "Bluegrass" began near here, and its pleasant sounds of blended guitar, mandolin, fiddle, and other stringed instruments are heard at the annual Bluegrass Music Festival of the U.S.A. It's held in this city, across the Ohio River from New Albany, Indiana.

8. Groundhog Day, February 2, is observed throughout the United States. The custom was brought here by settlers from England and Germany. But the nation's official Groundhog Day celebration is held in this Pennsylvania town. If the groundhog sees its shadow here, six more weeks of winter are in the forecast. The town is in Jefferson County, on Mahoning Creek, a few miles southeast of Walston and south of Anita. Its name begins with "P" and has 12 letters.

9. New Englanders have long based a large part of their diet and their culture on the sea. The Maine Seafood Festival is an event that celebrates both. It's held in this community on the west side of Penobscot Bay, the seat of Knox County. The name of the town beings with "R" and has eight letters.

10. The highlands of western Virginia were settled in the 1700s by people from the highlands of Scotland. In August, Scottish culture is celebrated by their descendents—and anyone else who cares to attend the Highlands Arts and Crafts Festival in this town. It's the seat of Washington County and is located about 115 miles southwest of Roanoke and about seven miles north of the Tennessee border. The name of the town has eight letters and ends with the letter "N."

Can you identify the sites of all of these festivals? Write the names of the cities and states on the lines below.

1. _____   6. _____

2. _____   7. _____

3. _____   8. _____

4. _____   9. _____

5. _____   10. _____

Answer Key

Exploring the Northeastern States
Pages 8–10

1. Wilmington, DE
2. Atlantic City, NJ
3. New London, CT
4. Gloucester, MA
5. Portland, ME
6. Littleton, NH
7. Burlington, VT
8. Albany, NY
9. Lancaster, PA
10. Hershey, PA

A Southeastern Treasure Hunt
Pages 11–13

1. Petersburg, VA
2. Durham, NC
3. Charleston, SC
4. Columbus, GA
5. Tuskegee, AL
6. Mobile, AL
7. Baton Rouge, LA
8. Hot Springs, AR
9. Nashville, TN
10. Louisville, KY

In the Heart of the Country
Pages 14–16

1. Wheeling, WV
2. Milwaukee, WI
3. Sioux City, IA
4. Battle Creek, MI
5. Canton, OH
6. Terre Haute, IN
7. Minneapolis, MN
8. Cleveland, OH
9. Jefferson City, MO
10. Chicago, IL

Where the West Begins
Pages 17–19

1. Brownsville, TX
2. San Antonio, TX
3. Claremore, OK
4. Great Bend, KS
5. North Platte, NE
6. Rapid City, SD
7. Dickinson, ND
8. Billings, MT
9. Jackson, WY
10. Pocatello, ID

Ocean, Mountain, Desert: The Far West
Pages 20–22

1. Nome, AK
2. Honolulu, HI
3. Cortez, CO
4. Albuquerque, NM
5. Kingman, AZ
6. Las Vegas, NV
7. Cedar City, UT
8. San Francisco, CA
9. Ashland, OR
10. Tacoma, WA

Answer Key

Find the Monument
Pages 24–26

1. Cahokia, IL
2. St. Augustine, FL
3. Ninety Six, SC
4. Williamsburg, VA
5. Santa Fe, NM
6. Monmouth, NJ
7. Philadelphia, PA
8. Pittsburgh, PA
9. St. Ignace, MI
10. Chicago, IL

On the Trail of the Great and the Near-Great
Pages 27–29

1. Atlanta, GA
2. Memphis, TN
3. Rochester, NY
4. Auburn, NY
5. Taos, NM
6. Joseph, OR
7. Vicksburg, MS
8. Brunswick, ME
9. Baltimore, MD
10. Providence, RI

Finding Lily Lightfoot
Pages 30–32

1. Okeechobee, FL
2. New York, NY
3. Hillsboro, OH
4. Moorhead, MN
5. Window Rock, AZ
6. Tahlequah, OK
7. Tulsa, OK
8. Missoula, MT
9. Kennewick, WA
10. Juneau, AK

A Journey through Space and Time
Pages 33–35

1. Seneca Falls, NY
2. Placerville, CA
3. Harpers Ferry, WV
4. Abilene, KS
5. Dearborn, MI
6. Dayton, TN
7. Waipahu, HI
8. Montgomery, AL
9. Dallas, TX
10. Berkeley, CA

Answer Key

In the Wild
Pages 36–38

1. Lone Pine
2. Grand Junction
3. Scottsbluff
4. Cody
5. Anchorage
6. Bishop
7. Tucson
8. Corpus Christi
9. Cincinnati
10. Craig

Report from Planet Earth
Pages 39–41

1. Titusville, FL
2. Houston, TX
3. Huntsville, AL
4. Worcester, MA
5. Washington, DC
6. Lima, OH
7. Lancaster, CA
8. San Jose, CA
9. Flagstaff, AZ
10. Roswell, NM

Geography by the Numbers
Pages 42–44

1. Anaconda, MT
2. Bowling Green, KY
3. Canyon de Chelly, AZ
4. Dodge City, KS
5. Ely, MN
6. Fairbanks, AK
7. Green Bay, WI
8. Hilo, HI
9. Isle Royale, MI
10. Jacksonville, FL

Where to Film the Movie
Pages 45–47

1. Barrow, AK
2. Portland, OR
3. Boston, MA
4. Concord, MA
5. Springfield, MA
6. Meredith, NH
7. Yellow Springs, OH
8. Hannibal, MO
9. Rawlins, WY
10. De Smet, SD

Answer Key

In Search of the Perfect Meal
Pages 48–50

1. Kansas City, MO/KS
2. Indianola, MS
3. Newport, RI
4. St. Albans, VT
5. Detroit, MI
6. Wichita, KS
7. Twin Falls, ID
8. Honolulu, HI
9. San Diego, CA
10. San Bernardino, CA

Once Upon a Mountaintop
Pages 52–54

1. Mount McKinley
2. Kilauea
3. Mount Washington
4. Mount Mitchell
5. Frémont Peak
6. Pikes Peak
7. Mount Rushmore
8. Mount Whitney
9. Mount St. Helens
10. Driskill Mountain

A "Cross-Country" Swim
Pages 55–56

1. Missouri River
2. Great Salt Lake
3. East River
4. Reelfoot Lake
5. Colorado River
6. Crater Lake
7. Suwannee River
8. Flathead Lake
9. Murderkill River
10. Lake Winnebago

Capitals, West to East
Pages 57–59

1. Sacramento, CA
2. Carson City, NV
3. Salt Lake City, UT
4. Denver, CO
5. Lincoln, NE
6. Des Moines, IA
7. Springfield, IL
8. Frankfort, KY
9. Charleston, WV
10. Annapolis, MD

Answer Key

From the Mountains to the Prairies
Pages 60–62

1. Mojave Desert
2. Cascade Mountains
3. Llano Estacado
4. Black Hills
5. Sand Hills
6. Badlands
7. Ozark Plateau
8. Beaver Island
9. Blue Ridge Mountains
10. Okefenokee Swamp

Sidewinder Sue's Lost Treasure
Pages 64–66

1. Barstow
2. San Diego
3. Los Angeles
4. Santa Barbara
5. Fresno
6. Monterey
7. San Francisco
8. Stockton
9. Eureka
10. Nevada City

On the Trail of Lightfingers Louie
Pages 67–69

1. Maine
2. New York
3. Virginia
4. North Carolina
5. Tennessee
6. Missouri
7. Kansas
8. Colorado
9. New Mexico
10. Arizona

The Stolen Wedding Ring
Pages 70–72

1. Texas
2. El Paso
3. Odessa
4. Lubbock
5. Amarillo
6. Austin
7. San Antonio
8. Galveston
9. Fort Worth
10. Texarkana

The Empire State Caper
Pages 73–74

1. Brooklyn
2. Staten Island
3. Albany
4. Troy
5. Lake Placid
6. Oswego
7. Syracuse
8. Ithaca
9. Buffalo
10. Niagara Falls

Map Mysteries
© The Learning Works, Inc.

Answer Key

Inventions, East to West
Pages 76–78
1. Boston, MA
2. New York, NY
3. Philadelphia, PA
4. Cleveland, OH
5. Louisville, KY
6. Shelbyville, IL
7. De Kalb, IL
8. St. Louis, MO
9. Beaver, UT
10. San Francisco, CA

In the Wilderness
Pages 79–81
1. Yosemite
2. Mount Rainier
3. Glacier
4. Yellowstone
5. Rocky Mountain
6. Bryce Canyon
7. Grand Canyon
8. Voyageurs
9. Great Smoky Mountains
10. Everglades

The Honored and Remembered
Pages 82–84
1. Arlington, VA
2. Dunseith, ND
3. New York, NY
4. Baltimore, MD
5. Evansville, IN
6. Montgomery, AL
7. Enterprise, AL
8. St. Martinsville, LA
9. Lewiston, ID
10. Casper, WY

Mystery Locations: Sports
Pages 85–87
1. Shelby, MT
2. Wendover, UT
3. Aspen, CO
4. Omaha, NE
5. South Bend, IN
6. Ann Arbor, MI
7. Springfield, MA
8. Hoboken, NJ
9. Latrobe, PA
10. Williamsport, PA

Meet Me at the Festival
Pages 88–90
1. Los Angeles, CA
2. Pendleton, OR
3. Gallup, NM
4. Beaumont, TX
5. New Orleans, LA
6. Davenport, IA
7. Louisville, KY
8. Punxsutawney, PA
9. Rockland, ME
10. Abingdon, VA